Microwave
Miracles

FROM

Microwave Miracles

FROM

With grateful thanks to Deirdre O'Callaghan and Lynne Creek who supplied the recipes for this cook book.

Contents

WHAT'S IT ALL ABOUT?

Welcome to the exciting world of Sanyo microwave cooking. You are joining the countless thousands of people who have discovered the joys of using Sanyo microwave ovens and will be delighted in this fast, easy, and efficient method of cooking. But, as with any new appliance, before you start using it you should take time to read the instructions carefully. The illustrated introductory chapters will show and tell you all about the way the oven works, why it works that way, what it can do, and how to get the most out of it. There is nothing complicated about using the oven; all you need is a little understanding of the special qualities of microwave cooking and you'll be on your way. Like any comprehensive conventional cookbook, this book tries to leave nothing to chance, so that cooking in the microwave oven will be as easy as it looks. Whether you plan to use the microwave for all of your cooking or only part of it, take a few minutes to familiarize yourself with the principles and techniques of the oven, then try the wonderful recipes in the chapters that follow. You'll soon find you'll never want to cook any other way but the microwave way.

To install your oven, follow the manufacturer's directions. A microwave oven operates on standard local voltage household current.

Your microwave oven will require little maintenance. Again, follow your manufacturer's directions for the few simple cleaning steps. Unlike a conventional oven, which generates heat in the oven cavity, there is no heat in the microwave cavity, so food and grease do not bake on. No harsh cleaning agents or difficult cleaning tasks are necessary. Just a simple wiping is all you need to keep the oven clean.

Keep the door and gasket free of food buildup to maintain a tight seal. Now, let's find out how the microwave oven works.

How Does It Work?

In conventional cooking by gas or electricity, food on top of the stove cooks by heat applied to the bottom of the pan, and in the oven by hot air, which surrounds the food. In microwave cooking, microwaves travel directly to the food, without heating the oven. Inside the top of the microwave oven is a magnetron vacuum tube, which converts ordinary electrical energy into high-frequency microwaves, just like radio and television waves. A fan-like device called a stirrer helps distribute the microwaves evenly throughout the oven. Microwaves are waves of energy, not heat. They are either reflected, pass through, or are absorbed, depending upon the material contacted. For example, metal reflect microwaves; glass, pottery, paper, and most plastics allow the waves to pass through; and, finally, food absorbs microwaves. Very simply then, the absorbed microwave energy causes the food molecules to vibrate rapidly against each other, inducing friction, which in turn produces the heat that cooks the food. This is somewhat like the way heat is generated when you rub your hands together. The waves penetrate the food, and cooking begins from the exterior. The interior then cooks by conduction. The prime rib photo on next page illustrates this principle. This process produces the much-appreciated cooking speed of the microwave oven. Because the cooking containers used in the microwave oven do not absorb microwave energy, they do not become hot. The microwaves pass through the containers directly into the food. However, the containers may absorb heat from the food itself, so you will occasionally need to use ovengloves. The see-through panel in the microwave oven door is made of a specially prepared material that contains a metal screen. The metal screen reflects the microwaves, yet enables you to observe the food as it cooks. The waves cannot penetrate this screen. Opening the microwave oven door turns the unit off automatically, so you can stir, turn, or check cooking with ease. And you don't have to face that blast of hot air you expect when opening a conventional oven.

Now that you've learned something about how the microwave oven works, let's take a look at all the wonderful things you can do with it.

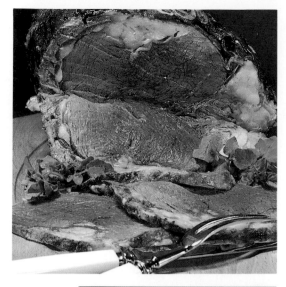

LOOK WHAT YOU CAN DO!

You can cook just about anything in the microwave oven, but some foods are so especially good done this way that we want to show several of them to you. You'll find that the microwave oven not only cooks food superbly from scratch, but also reheats and defrosts with excellent results. Let's take a look.

□ *Roast beef* is juicy and rare, with less shrinkage than in the conventional oven. □ You can enjoy all kinds of *vegetables* at their wholesome best. Their true flavour and colour are preserved. Potatoes are fluffy, cauliflower crisp, and broccoli the beautiful green it was born with. □ You'll want *scrambled eggs* for breakfast, lunch, and supper when you've tried them microwave-style. They're fluffier than in conventional cooking, and more pleasing to the eye as well as the palate.

□ You'll think positively about *leftovers* after you try them reheated in the microwave. Food will have that justcooked taste and look.

□ Cook luscious *chocolate cakes,* so tantalizingly moist, rich, and light. □ *Fruit,* such as this baked apple, can be prepared without water; like vegetables, fruit retains that just-picked colour and flavour. □ *Sauces* are a blessing to cook in the microwave oven. Constant stirring is a thing of the past. Just imagine the convenience of mixing, cooking, and serving all in the same container. Hollandaise sauce is smooth with just a few stirrings. □ The microwave can't be beaten for *heating rolls and bread* so quickly they don't have a chance to be anything but perfect. And you can cook them right in the serving basket as long as there are no metal fasteners or trim.

□ *Bacon* cooked in the microwave is incomparable—flat and crisp—and one slice takes less than a minute to cook. It can be placed on a microproof bacon rack or between paper towels.
□ *Desserts* are a particular favourite for microwave cooks because they are as easy as pie. Chocolate and cara-melized mixtures won't require constant stirring. □ *Hot appetizers* are ready as needed, cooking quickly, with no mess and no pan to clean. Just cook them directly on paper plates or in a serving dish. □ *Casseroles* cook without sticking and are just as good served later.

☐ Explore the pleasures of cooking *seafood* in your microwave oven. Fish fillets and steaks are moist and tender, their natural juices enhancing their delicate flavour. ☐ And for a pick-me-up that's really quick there's no equal to a *bowl of soup,* a cup of coffee, or a mug of cocoa served directly from the oven. ☐ *Melt chocolate* and *soften butter or cream cheese* in seconds and save the time and mess of double boilers and burned pans.

Now that you've had a sample of what this appliance can do, let's take a look at what you need to know in order to start cooking.

HERE'S WHAT YOU NEED TO KNOW

In this chapter you will find everything you need to know to make microwave cooking easy, efficient, and pleasurable. Once you know the principles, the techniques will become second nature. Read this basic information with its accompanying illustrations carefully. As you begin to use the oven, you can always refer back to this handy guide whenever a question arises about a cooking term or method. Here you will learn why some foods cook faster than others, what you should know about timing and temperature, which cooking utensils are appropriate, how to cook most efficiently, and much more.

Because of the unique qualities of microwave energy, microwave cooking uses certain terms and methods that are different from those of conventional cooking. For example, in microwave cooking, many foods complete their cooking after being removed from the oven. This is known as standing time. In addition, how food is arranged in the cooking dish is important to its being cooked evenly throughout. You'll be introduced as well to the oven's facility to defrost and to reheat quickly, with special hints for best results.

ABOUT TIMING

Time is an important element in microwave cooking. But isn't that statement true for all cooking? You, the cook, have to be the judge, as you consider your family's preferences and use your own instincts. Chances are, you can tell if a chicken is done simply by looking at it. You might even scoff at the timing chart given on a package because you know that a particular food always seems to need more or less time. It is important to know that even though the microwave oven is a superb product of computer technology, it is no more or less precise than any other cooking system. Nevertheless, because of the speed with which most foods are cooked, timing is more crucial in microwave cooking than in conventional cooking. One minute can cause a significant difference. When you consider that a cooking task requiring one hour in a conventional oven generally needs only one-quarter of that time in a microwave oven, you can understand why microwave cooking requires a somewhat different approach to timing. Where an extra minute in conventional cooking is seldom critical, in microwave cooking one minute can be the difference between overcooked and undercooked foods. Remember that it is better to undercook and add more cooking time than to overcook — then it's too late.

Cooking times might be precise if a way could be found to guarantee that all foods would be exactly the same each time we cook them; if the Gas or Electricity Board would guarantee not to alter our source of power (there are frequent changes in the voltage levels reaching our homes); and if the size, form, and content of foods would be consistently the same. The fact is that one potato or one steak varies from another in density, moisture or fat content, shape, weight, and temperture. This is true of all food. The cook must be ready to adjust to the changes, to be flexible and observant. This discussion really comes down to the fact that you, not the microwave oven, are the cook. The oven can't make judgments, so you must. The recipes in this book have all been meticulously kitchen tested by expert home economists. As in all fine cooking, however, microwave cooking needs and benefits from your personal touch.

ABOUT FOOD CHARACTERISTICS

Food is made up of distinct elements that specifically affect timing in microwave cooking. Understanding these important qualities will help you become a skilled and successful microwave cook.

Quantity

The larger the volume of food there is, the more time is needed to cook it. For example, one potato may cook in 4 to 6 minutes but 2 potatoes take about one and a half times as long. One ear of corn in the husk cooks in about 3 minutes where 3 ears may cook in 8 minutes. Therefore, if the quantity in a recipe is changed, be sure to make an adjustment in timing. When increasing a recipe, increase the amount of cooking time. Here is a general rule to follow: When doubling a recipe, increase the cooking time approximately 50 percent. When cutting a recipe in half, reduce the time by approximately 40 percent.

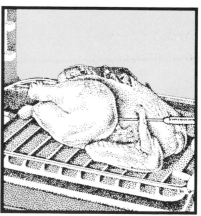

*Moist food cooks faster than dry (left).
Frozen food takes longer to cook than
canned (center). A sweet roll heats a bit
faster than a dinner roll (right).*

Shape and Size

Thin food cooks faster than thick food;
thin sections faster than thick. Small
pieces also cook faster than large
pieces. For even cooking, place thick
pieces toward the outside of the dish
since the outside areas cook faster than
the inside areas. For best results, try to
cook pieces of similar size and shape
together.

Height

As in conventional cooking, areas that
are closer to the energy source cook
faster. In most microwave ovens, the
energy source is at the top of the oven.
Food close to the top may require
shielding with pieces of aluminum foil
or turning for even cooking.

Density

Dense foods like potatoes, roast beef,
and carrots take longer to cook than
porous foods, such as cakes, ground
beef, and apples, because it takes the
microwaves longer to penetrate the
denser texture. For example, a 2-pound
roast will take longer than a 2-pound
meat loaf.

Moisture Content

Moist food cooks faster than dry food
because microwave energy is easily
absorbed by the moisture within the
food. For example, 1 cup of sliced
courgette will cook faster than 1 cup of
carrots because of the high water
content in the courgette. In fact, the
amount of free moisture within a food
helps determine how rapidly it cooks.

Delicate Ingredients

This term is used to refer to food that
cooks so quickly in the microwave
oven that it can overcook — toughening,
separating, or curdling. For example,
mayonnaise, cheese, eggs, cream,
dairy sour cream, etc. Other food may
"pop," such as snails, oysters, and
chicken livers. For this reason, a lower
power setting is often recommended
for proper cooking. However, when
these ingredients are mixed with other
food, as in a casserole, stew, or soup,
you may use a higher power setting,
because volume automatically slows
down the cooking.

Sugar and Fat Content

Food high in sugar and fat heats quicker than items low in these ingredients, because microwave energy is attracted by sugar and fat. For example, the fruit or cheese filling of a sweet roll will heat faster than the roll itself and will be hotter, since sugar and fat reach higher temperatures than food low in sugar or fat content.

Starting Temperature

As in conventional cooking, the temperature at which food is placed in the microwave oven affects the length of cooking time. More time is needed to cook food just out of the refrigerator than food at room temperature. For example, it takes longer to heat frozen green beans than canned green beans. Also, hot tap water will start boiling sooner than cold. Recipes in this book assume that food is at refrigerator temperature.

ABOUT UTENSILS

A wide variety of cookware and cooking implements can be used in the microwave oven. In order to indicate an item made of material that is safe and recommended for microwave cooking, we have created a new term, *microproof.* The Materials Checklist and Microproof Utensils Chart on the following pages will aid you in selecting the appropriate microproof utensil. Except for metal, most materials are microproof for a limited amount of cooking time. But unless specifically approved, items made of metal, even partially, are never to be used in the microwave oven, because they reflect microwaves, preventing them from passing through the cooking utensil into the food. In addition, metal that touches the oven sides will cause sparks, a static charge, known as arcing.

Arcing is not harmful to you, though it deface the oven. Metal twist ties or dishes or cups with gold or silver trim should not be used. See the Materials Checklist for those approved types of metal, such as pieces of aluminum foil, used as a shield over certain areas of food to prevent overcooking, or metal clips attached to frozen turkey.

When selecting a new piece of cookware, first check the manufacturer's directions. Also review the Materials Checklist and the Guide to Microproof Cookware. If you are still in doubt, try this test: Pour a cup of water into an ovenproof glass measure and place in the oven next to the container or dish to be tested. Cook on High for 1 minute. If the new dish feels hot, don't use it—it is absorbing microwave energy. If it feels warm, the dish may only be used for warming food. If it remains at room temperature, it is *microproof.*

The rapid growth of microwave cooking has created many new products for use in the microwave oven. Among these are microproof replacements for cookware formerly available only in metal. You'll find a wide variety at your store—cake, muffin pans, roasting racks, etc. When you add these to traditional microproof cookware and the incredible array of microproof plastic and paper products, you'll find that microwave cooking enables you to select from many more kinds of cookware than are available for conventional cooking.

Unique roasting racks, browning dishes, and other cookware have been developed for microwave use (top left). Familiar items, such as mould and muffin pans, are now available in microproof materials (top right). A wide variety of glass, ceramic, and wood items are perfect for microwave use (above right). All kinds of paper products make microwave cooking especially easy (above left). Many plastics are safe for microwave use (left).

Selecting Containers

Containers should accommodate the food being cooked. Whenever possible use round or oval dishes, so that the microwaves are absorbed evenly into the food. Square corners in cookware receive more concentration of energy than the rest of the dish, so the food in the corners tends to overcook. Some cake and loaf recipes call for ring moulds to facilitate more even cooking. This is because the centre area in a round or oval dish generally cooks more slowly than the outside. Round cookware with a small glass inserted open end up in the centre works just as well to eliminate undercooked centre. When a particular size or shape of container is specified in a recipe, it should be used. Varying the container size or shape may change cooking time. A 2-quart casserole called for in a recipe refers to a bowl-shaped cooking utensil. A 12×8-inch or a 9-inch round baking dish refers to a shallow cooking dish. In the case of puddings, sauces, and desserts, large containers are specified to prevent the liquids, especially milkbased ones, from boiling over. For best results, try to use the dish cited in the recipe.

Materials Checklist

☐ CHINA, POTTERY: Ideal for microwave use. However, if they have metallic trim or glaze, they are not microproof and should not be used.

☐ GLASS: An excellent microwave cooking material. Especially useful for baking pies to check pastry cases through the bottom. Since ovenproof glass is always safe, "microproof" is not mentioned in any recipe where a glass item is specified.

☐ METALS: *Not* suitable except as follows:

Small strips of aluminum foil can be used to cover areas on large pieces of meat or poultry that defrost or cook more rapidly than the rest of the piece — for example, a roast with jagged areas or thin ends, or the wing or breast bone of poultry. This method is known as shielding in microwave cooking.

Shallow aluminum frozen TV dinner trays with foil covers removed can be heated, provided that the trays do not exceed 3/4 inch depth. (However, TV dinners heat much faster if you "pop" the blocks of food out and arrange them on microproof dinner plates.)

Frozen poultry containing metal clamps may be defrosted in the microwave oven without removing the clamps. Remove the clamps after defrosting.

Trays or any foil or metal item must be at least 1 inch from oven walls.

☐ PAPER: Approved for short-term cooking and for reheating at low settings. These must not be foil-lined. Extended use may cause the paper to burn. Grease proof paper is a suitable covering.

☐ PLASTICS: May be used if dishwasher safe, but only for limited cooking periods or for heating. Do not use plastics for tomato-based food or food with high fat or high sugar content.

☐ PLASTIC COOKING BAGS: Can be used. Slit the bag so steam can escape.

☐ STRAW AND WOOD: Can be used for quick warming. Be certain no metal is used on the straw or wood items.

Browning Dish

A browning dish is used to sear, grill, fry, or brown food. It is made to absorb microwave energy when the dish is preheated empty. A special coating on the bottom of the dish becomes very hot when preheated in the microwave oven. There are a variety of dishes available. Follow the manufacturer's instructions for care and use and for the length of time to preheat the dish.

After the dish is preheated, vegetable oil or butter may be added to enhance the browning and prevent food from sticking. After the food is placed on the preheated browning dish, the dish is returned to the oven, where the microwaves cook the interior of the food while the hot surface of the dish browns the exterior. The food is then turned over to brown the other side. When cooking hamburger or moist foods, you may wish to pour off accumulated juices before turning the food over. The longer you wait to turn the food the less browning occurs, since the dish cools off rapidly. You may need to drain the dish, wipe it out, and preheat it again. In doubling a recipe, such as fried chicken, wipe out the browning dish after the first batch, reheat the empty dish, and repeat the procedure. Since the browning dish becomes very hot, be sure to use oven gloves when handling it.

Used as a grill, the browning dish speeds cooking time. However, if you wish to use the dish to brown certain foods prior to adding them to a recipe, your recipe time will remain about the same. Some foods, such as eggs or sandwiches, require less heat for browning than other foods, such as chicken or meat.

A GUIDE TO MICROPROOF COOKWARE

ITEM	GOOD USE	GENERAL NOTES
China plates, cups	Heating dinners and drinks.	No metal trim.
Cooking pouches (plastic)	Cooking meat, vegetables, rice, other frozen food.	Slit pouch so steam can escape.
Corning Ware" or Pyrex casseroles	Cooking main dishes, vegetables, desserts.	No metal trim.
Microwave browning dishes or grills	Searing, grilling, and frying small meat items; grilling sandwiches; frying eggs.	These utensils are specially made to absorb microwaves and preheat to high temperatures. They brown food that otherwise would not brown in a microwave oven.
Microwave roasting racks	Cooking roasts and chickens, and potatoes.	Special racks are available for cooking bacon.
Oven film and cooking bags	Cooking roasts or stews.	Substitute string for metal twist ties. Bag itself will not cause tenderizing. Do not use film with foil edges.
Paper plates, cups, napkins	Heating hot dogs, drinks, rolls, appetizers, sandwiches.	Absorbs moisture from baked goods and freshens them. Paper plates and cups with wax coatings should not be used.
Plastic wrap	Covering dishes.	Fold back edge to ventilate, allowing steam to escape.
Pottery and earthenware plates, mugs, etc.	Heating dinners, soups, drinks.	Some pottery has a metallic glaze. To check, use dish test (page 9).
Soft plastics, cartons	Reheating leftovers.	Used for very short reheating periods.
Thermometers	Measuring temperature of meat, poultry, and sweets.	Use only approved microproof meat or sugar thermometer in microwave oven.
TV dinner trays (aluminum)	Frozen dinners or homemade dinners.	No deeper than $\frac{3}{4}$ inch. Food will receive heat from top surface only. Foil covering food must be removed.
Grease proof paper	Covering casseroles. Use as a tent.	Prevents splattering. Helps contain heat where a tight seal is not required.
Wooden spoons, wooden skewers, straw baskets	Stirring puddings and sauces; for shish kebabs, appetizers, warming breads.	Can withstand microwaves for short cooking periods. Be sure no metal fittings on wood or straw.

Microwave arrangement methods create unique cook-and-serve opportunities. The cauliflower and broccoli dish, for example, is cooked, covered, for 9 minutes on HIGH with ¼ cup water.

ABOUT METHODS

The evenness and speed of microwave cooking are affected not only by the characteristics of the food itself, but also by certain methods, described below. Some of these techniques are used in conventional cooking as well, but they have a particular application in microwave cooking because of the special qualities of microwave energy. Many other important variables that influence cooking, defrosting, and reheating in the microwave oven are included here. Becoming familiar with these terms and methods will make microwave cooking easy and successful.

Arrangement

The way food is arranged on the cooking surface helps ensure evenness and facilitates speed in defrosting, heating, and cooking food. The microwaves penetrate the outer portion of food first; therefore, food should be arranged so that the denser, thicker areas are near the edge, and the thinner, more porous areas are near the centre. For example, when cooking broccoli, split the heavy stalks to expose more area, then overlap with flowerets; or you can alternate flowerets of cauliflower with broccoli for an attractive dish. This gives even density to the food and provides even cooking. Place shrimp in a ring with the tails toward the centre. Chicken legs should be arranged like the spokes of a wheel, with the bony end toward the centre. Food such as fairy cakes, tomatoes, and potatoes should be arranged in a circle, rather than in rows.

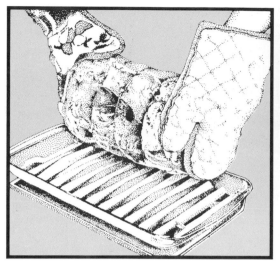

Turning Over

As in conventional cooking, some food, such as large roasts, whole poultry, a ham, or hamburgers, may require turning over to brown each side and to promote even heating. Any food seared on the browning dish should be turned over. During the defrosting process in the microwave oven, it is often necessary to turn the food.

Rearranging

Sometimes food that cannot be stirred needs repositioning in the cooking utensil to allow even heating throughout. When rearranging food, move the centre food to the outside of the dish and the outer food toward the centre.

Stirring

Less stirring is required in microwave cooking than in conventional cooking. When necessary, stir from the outside to the centre since the outside heats faster than the centre portion. Stirring blends the flavour and promotes even heating. Stir only as directed in the recipes. Constant stirring is never required in microwave cooking.

Rotating

A few foods, such as pies and cakes, that cannot be stirred, turned over, or rearranged call for repositioning the cooking dish one-quarter turn to allow for even distribution of the microwave energy. Rotate only if the baked food is not cooking or rising evenly. Most food does not need to be rotated.

A one-quarter rotation is used for some muffins and cakes (above left). Covers are as important in microwave cooking as in conventional (left and above).

Covering

Covers are used to trap steam, prevent dehydration, speed cooking time, and help food retain its natural moisture. Suitable tight coverings are microproof casserole tops, glass covers, plastic wraps, oven bags, and microproof plates and saucers. Boilable freezer bags may be used as containers for the frozen food inside. Pierce top with a knife to ventilate before cooking. Remove coverings away from your face to prevent steam burns. Paper toweling is especially useful as a light covering to prevent splatter and to absorb moisture.

Shielding

Certain thin or bony areas, such as the wing tips of poultry, the head and tail of fish, or the breastbone of a turkey, cook faster than thicker areas. Covering these part with small pieces of aluminum foil shields these areas from overcooking, since aluminum foil reflects the waves. Besides preventing thin parts of food from cooking more rapidly than thicker ones, shielding may be used during defrosting to cover those portions that

defrost more quickly than others. Use aluminum foil only when recommended in recipes. Be careful not to allow the foil to touch the oven walls.

Standing Time

This term refers to the time food needs to complete cooking after being removed from the microwave oven. During standing time, heat continues to be conducted from the outside to the centre of the food. After the oven is turned off, food may remain in the oven for standing time or may be placed on a heatproof counter. This procedure is an essential part of food preparation with the microwave oven. Some food, such as roasts, requires standing time to attain the proper internal temperature for rare, medium, or well-done levels. Casseroles need standing time to allow the heat to spread evenly and to complete reheating or cooking. With cakes, pies, and quiches, standing time permits the centre to finish cooking. During the standing time outside the oven, place food on a flat surface, such as a heat-resistant bread board or counter top, not on a cooling rack as you would conventionally.

Piercing

It is necessary to break the skin or membrane of certain food, such as egg yolks, potatoes, liver, chicken giblets, and eggplant. Because the skins or membranes retain moisture during cooking, they must be pierced before cooking to prevent bursting and to allow steam to escape. For example, pierce sausage casing in several places before cooking. A toothpick may be used for egg yolks; a fork is best for potatoes; a knife is best to slit plastic cooking bags.

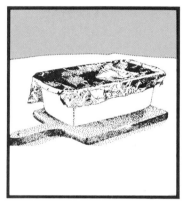

Piercing (above right). The effect of standing time on roast beef (right). Use a flat surface for standing time (above).

Browning

Many foods do not brown in the microwave oven as much as they do in the conventional oven. Depending upon the fat content, most food will brown in 8 to 10 minutes in the microwave oven. For example, bacon browns in minutes because of its high fat content, but poultry will not brown even after 10 minutes. For food that cooks too quickly to brown, such as hamburgers, fried eggs, steak or cutlets, a special browning dish is available. The longer the cooking time, or the higher the fat content, the more browning will be achieved. You can also create a browned look on roasts, poultry, steaks, and other foods by brushing on a browning agent, such as gravy mix, soy sauce, dehydrated onion soup mix, paprika, etc. Cakes, bread, and pie shells do not brown as they do in conventional cooking. Using chocolate, spices, or dark flour helps attain the dark colour. Otherwise, you can create appealing colour by adding frostings, toppings, or glazes.

GETTING TO KNOW YOUR OVEN

Your microwave oven gives you the ability to select from many power settings in graduated form from 10 to 100 percent—HI (max. power). Just as in a conventional oven, these settings give you flexibility and the necessary control to produce perfectly cooked dishes. You can set your multi-power oven to suit the food being cooked. Many foods require slow cooking at less than full power to achieve the best results. Each recipe in the book indicates which power setting is recommended for the food being cooked. The following chart outlines the specific uses for the main settings.

Reheating
One of the major assets of the microwave oven is its efficiency in reheating cooked food. Not only does most food reheat quickly, but it also retains moisture and its just-cooked flavour when properly arranged and covered. If someone is late for dinner, there's no need to fret. Just place a microproof plate containing the cooked food in your oven; in moments, dinner is ready once again. Reheat food in serving dishes or on paper plates and save extra clean-up time. Take-away food, which usually arrives at your home cold off, can be

Guide for Cook Control Settings

Main Setting		Suggested Cooking Uses
LOW	(10%)	Softening cream cheese; keeping casseroles and main dishes warm.
WARM	(20%)	Softening chocolate; heating breads, rolls, pancakes, tacos, tortillas, and French toast; clarifying butter; taking chill out of fruit; heating small amounts of food.
DEFROST	(30—35%)	Thawing meat, poultry and seafood; finish cooking casseroles, stews, and some sauces; cooking small quantities of most food.
BRAISE	(40%)	Cooking less tender cuts of meat in liquid and slow cooking dishes; finish cooking less tender roasts.
SIMMER	(50—55%)	Cooking stews and soups after bringing to the boil; cooking baked custards and pasta.
BAKE	(60%)	Cooking scrambled eggs; cakes.
ROAST	(70%)	Cooking rump roast, ham, veal, and lamb; cooking cheese dishes; cooking eggs, and milk; cooking quick breads and cereal products.
REHEAT	(80—85%)	Quickly reheating precooked or prepared food; heating sandwiches.
SAUTE	(90%)	Quickly cooking onions, celery, and green peppers; reheating meat slices quickly.
HIGH (cook)	(100%)	Cooking tender cuts of meat; cooking poultry, fish, vegetables, and most casseroles; preheating the browning dish; boiling water; thickening some sauces; cooking muffins.

Note; Cooking times given in this book are basically for electronic ranges with 600 watts output power.
Therefore, those who possess ranges with 500 watts output add on approx 20 percents of stated time. (EG. Cook book states 5 mins, actually cook for 6 mins. Cook book states 20 mins, actually cook for 24 mins.)
650-700 watts reduce stated time by approx 8 percents-15 percents. (EG. Cook book states 5 mins, actually cook for 4½-4¼ mins, cook book states 20 mins, actually cook for 18½-17 mins.)
All cooking times given are approximate, and intended as a guide only, since they will be affected by various factors such as starting temperature, density, thickness and quality of the food, as well as the size, type and shape of dish used and of course personal taste.
Always underestimate working time and test food readiness, to prevent overcooking.

easily reheated in seconds to its original state in your microwave oven. No more cold pizzas! Or lukewarm hamburgers. Leftovers are a treat too. You may even want to prepare food the day before, refrigerate, and serve the following day. You'll no longer call food leftovers, because it will taste as if "just made." Follow the tips below to help get excellent results when you are reheating food.

☐ To arrange a combination of different foods on a plate, place the dense food, like meat, at the outer edges and the more porous food, like breads, toward the centre. Food that cooks most quickly should be placed at the centre, with slower cooking food at the edges.

☐ Dense food, such as mashed potatoes and casseroles, cooks more quickly and evenly if a depression is made in the centre, or if the food is shaped in a ring.

☐ To retain moisture during reheating, cover food with plastic wrap or a microproof lid. Wrap breads, pies and sandwiches in paper toweling to absorb moisture and prevent sogginess.

☐ Spread food out in a shallow container rather than piling it high, for quicker and more even heating.

☐ As a general guide to reheating a plate of food start with 1½ to 2 minutes, then check. If the plate on which the food is cooked feels warm the food is probably heated through, since its warmth has heated the plate. Because of the numerous variables in the food to be reheated, i.e., amount, shape, food characteristics, starting temperature, etc., recommended heating times can only be approximate.

Defrosting

One of the great attractions of the microwave oven is its ability to defrost raw food or heat frozen cooked food. You need only to set the oven at defrost for most food and observe the swiftness and ease of defrosting almost any food.

Many of the same principles and techniques that apply to microwave cooking also apply to microwave defrosting and heating. Microwaves are attracted to water or moisture molecules. As soon as microwaves have defrosted a portion of the item they are more attracted to the thawed portion. The frozen portion continues to thaw, but this is due to the heat in the thawed portion. Special techniques, such as shielding and rotating, are helpful to be sure the thawed portion does not cook before the rest defrosts. It is often necessary to turn, stir, and separate to assist the defrosting process. Defrosting requires standing time to complete. Because food differs in size, weight, and density, recommended defrosting times can only be approximate. Additional standing time may be necessary to defrost completely. Here are some tips to aid you toward fast and easy defrosting:

Defrost most food in its original wrapper (above left). Thawed portions of ground beef (above) are removed from the oven so cooking does not start. Fish fillets (far left) are separated as soon as possible. Many foods are turned over during defrosting (left).

☐ Poultry, seafood, fish, meat, and most vegetables may be defrosted in their original closed package. You may leave metal clips in poultry during defrosting, but you should remove them as soon as possible before cooking. Replace metal twists on bags with string or rubber bands before defrosting.

☐ Poultry wings, legs, and the small or bony ends of meat or fish may need to be covered with pieces of aluminum foil for part of the thawing time to prevent cooking while the remainder thaws.

☐ Large items should be turned and rotated halfway through defrosting time to provide more even thawing.

☐ Food textures influence thawing time. Because of air space, porous foods like cake and bread defrost more quickly than a solid mass, such as a sauce, or roast.

☐ Do not thaw food wrapped in aluminum or in foil dishes except as approved.

☐ The edges will begin cooking if meat, fish, and seafood are completely thawed in the microwave oven. Therefore, food should still be icy in the centre when removed from oven. It will finish thawing while standing.

☐ Remove portions of ground meat as soon as thawed, returning frozen portions to the oven.

☐ To thaw half of a frozen vegetable package, wrap half the package with aluminum foil. When unwrapped side is thawed, separate and return balance to freezer.

☐ Thin or sliced items, such as fish fillets, meat patties, etc., should be separated as soon as possible. Remove thawed pieces and allow others to continue thawing.

☐ Casseroles, saucy food, vegetables, and soups should be stirred once or twice during defrosting to redistribute heat.

☐ Frozen fried food may be defrosted but will not be crisp when heated in the microwave oven.

☐ Freezing tips: It is helpful to freeze in small quantities rather than in one large piece. When freezing casseroles, it's a good idea to insert an empty paper cup in the centre so no food is present there. This speeds thawing. Depressing the centre of ground meat when freezing also hastens thawing later. Take care to wrap and package food well to retain its original quality. The wrapped food should be air-free, with air-tight seals. Store at −18°C/0°F or less for no longer than the times recommended for freezing.

By the Way...

To get the greatest pleasure out of your microwave oven, keep in mind that certain food is best done by conventional means of cooking. For the following reasons we don't recommend:

☐ Eggs cooked in the shell, because the light membrane surrounding the yolk collects energy, which then causes a steam build-up that could explode the egg.

☐ Deep-fat frying, because the confined environment of the oven is not suited to the handling of the food or oil and is not safe.

☐ Pancakes, because no crust forms. (But the oven is great for reheating pancakes, waffles, and similar items.)

☐ Toasting, because it also requires crust development.

☐ Home canning, because it is impossible to judge exact boiling temperatures inside jar and you cannot be sure that the temperature and length of cooking are sufficient to prevent contamination of the food.

☐ Chiffon and angel food cakes, because they require steady, dry heat to rise and be tender.

☐ Heating bottles with small necks, like those for syrups and toppings, because they are apt to break from the pressure build-up.

☐ Large items, such as a 25-pound turkey, because the space is not adequate.

Finally, about popcorn:

Do not attempt to pop corn in a paper bag, since the corn may dehydrate and overheat, causing the paper bag to catch fire. Due to the many variables, such as the age of the corn and its moisture content, popping corn in the microwave oven is not recommended.

ON YOUR OWN

You will undoubtedly want to cook some of your favourite conventional recipes in the microwave oven. With a little thought and experimenting you can convert many recipes. Before converting a recipe, study it to determine if it will adapt well to microwave cooking. Look for a recipe in the book that matches your conventional one most closely. For example, find a recipe with the same amount, type, and form of main ingredient, such as 1 pound ground meat or 2 pounds beef cut in 1-inch pieces, etc. Then compare other ingredients, such as pasta or vegetables. The microwave recipe will probably call for less liquid, because there is so little evaporation in microwave cooking. Use the following guidelines:

☐ Meatloaf, and certain baked goods may not need adjustments in ingredients. In sauces, gravies, and some casseroles, liquids should be reduced.

☐ Many casseroles will require adjustment in the order in which ingredients are added. Certain ingredients, such as uncooked rice, in a conventional recipe take longer to cook than others. When converting to the microwave, substitute a quicker-cooking ingredient, such as precooked rice. For example, substitute instant onion flakes for chopped onion, and cut vegetable ingredients, such as carrots, in smaller pieces than the conventional recipe recommends.

☐ Most converted recipes will require adjustments in cooking time. Although a "rule of thumb" always has exceptions, you can generally assume that most microwave recipes are heated in about one-quarter to one-third of the conventional recipe time. Check after one-quarter of the time before continuing to cook.

Now let's try converting a conventional recipe to the microwave oven. Suppose you have a favourite recipe for Chicken Marengo that you would like to prepare in your microwave oven.

Chicken Marengo
Conventional Style
4 to 6 servings

½	cup flour
1	teaspoon salt
½	teaspoon pepper
1	teaspoon tarragon
1	chicken, 3 pounds, cut up
¼	cup olive oil
¼	cup butter
1	cup dry white wine
2	cups canned tomatoes
1	clove garlic, finely chopped
8	mushrooms (½ pound), sliced
	Chopped parsley

Preheat oven to 350° F. Mix flour, salt, pepper, and tarragon, and dredge chicken with seasoned flour. Reserve remaining flour.

In skillet heat oil and butter, and brown chicken. Place chicken in large casserole. Add reserved flour to the fat in skillet and, using a wire whisk, gradually stir in wine. When sauce is thickened and smooth, pour over the chicken and add the tomatoes, garlic, and mushrooms. Cover casserole and bake until chicken is tender, about 45 minutes. Before serving sprinkle with parsley.

Checking the Chicken Marengo recipe, you'll notice that the amount of liquid is quite a bit less than in the conventional Chicken Marengo recipe. That's because liquids do not reduce in microwave cooking and we don't want a thin sauce. Notice, too, that the onion is cooked first to be sure it is tender and that the flavour of the dish is fully developed. In converting, the Chicken Marengo recipe, the liquid has reduced and the garlic is cooked first. Since the volume of food is about the same, the cooking times and power settings for Chicken Marengo are followed for Chicken Marengo Microwave Style. Here's the fully converted recipe:

Chicken Marengo
Microwave Style
4 to 6 servings

1	chicken, 3 pounds, cut up
1	teaspoon salt
½	teaspoon pepper
1	teaspoon tarragon
1	clove garlic, minced
1	tablespoon butter
1	tablespoon olive oil
¼	cup flour
½	cup dry white wine
2	cups canned tomatoes
8	mushrooms (½ pound), sliced
	Chopped parsley

Rub chicken with salt, pepper, and tarragon and set aside: Place garlic, butter, and olive oil in 3-quart microproof casserole. Cook, covered, on HIGH 1 minute. Add flour, stir until smooth, gradually adding wine. Stir in tomatoes and mushrooms. Cook, covered, on HIGH 5 minutes, stir. Add chicken, immersing pieces in sauce. Cook, covered, on HIGH 25 to 30 minutes, or until chicken is fork tender. Taste for seasoning, sprinkle with chopped parsley, and allow to stand covered 5 minutes before serving.
Butter, olive oil, and flour have been reduced since browning is not part of the microwave recipe. If you wish, however, add more butter and olive oil, dredge chicken in flour, and brown chicken in preheated browning dish. The white wine has been reduced to avoid a too thin sauce.

Cooking Casseroles
The microwave oven is exceptionally good for cooking casseroles. Vegetables keep their bright fresh colour and crisp texture. Meats are tender and full of flavour. Here are some general hints to help you:

☐ Most casseroles can be made ahead of time, refrigerated or frozen, then reheated later in the microwave.

☐ Casseroles are usually covered with plastic wrap or glass lids during cooking.

☐ Allow casseroles to stand 5 to 10 minutes before serving, according to size. Standing time allows the centre of the casserole to complete cooking.

☐ You will obtain best results if you make ingredients uniform in size, stirring occasionally to distribute heat. If the ingredients are of different sizes, stir more often.

☐ Casseroles containing less tender meat need longer simmering on a lower power setting. Casseroles with delicate ingredients such as cream or cheese sauces often need a lower setting. Cheese toppings added for the last 1 or 2 minutes should cook at a low setting also.

☐ When used in quick-cooking casseroles, celery, onions, green peppers, and carrots should be sautéed before being added to dish. Rice or noodles should be partially cooked before combining with cooked meat, fish, or poultry. Use higher power settings for these recipes.

OFF TO A GOOD START: APPETIZERS

Appetizers can be the most creative food of today's entertaining. They can be hot or cold, simple or fancy, light or hearty depending upon the occasion. There are no rules, so you can let your imagination soar. Until now *hot* appetizers were the most troublesome and time-consuming for the host or hostess. But that's no longer true with the microwave oven. Parties are much easier and more enjoyable because the microwave eliminates all that last-minute hassle and lengthy cooking over a hot stove. You can assemble most appetizers and nibbles in advance, and at the right moment, just coolly "heat 'n serve!" This chapter presents many recipes for entertaining your guests, but you'll also be tempted to prepare delicious snacks and munchies just for the family. There's no doubt about it — appetizers cooked in the microwave oven are fun to make, fun to serve, and fun to eat.

COOKING GUIDE—CONVENIENCE APPETIZERS

Food	Amount	Cook Control Setting	Time	Special Notes
Canned meat spread	4 oz.	Reheat	30-45 seconds	Transfer to small microproof bowl.
Canned sausages, cocktail sausages	5 oz.	Reheat	1½-2 minutes	Place in covered glass casserole.
Cocktail franks, pizza roll	4 servings	Roast	45-60 seconds	Place on paper towels. Roll will not crisp.
Cooked pizza, 10 inches, cut in 8 portions	1 wedge 4 wedges Whole	Reheat Reheat Roast	40-60 seconds 1½-2 minutes 3¼-4 minutes	Place on paper towels or paper plate or leave in uncovered cardboard box, points toward center.
Dips, cream	½ cup	Warm	1½-2½ minutes	Cover with plastic wrap.
Eggrolls, pastry-covered	2 servings	Roast	30-45 seconds	Place on paper towels, do not cover.
Swiss fondue, frozen	10 oz.	Reheat	5-6 minutes	Slit pouch. Place on microproof plate. Stir before serving.

HAM STUFFED TOMATOES
COOKING TIME 2½ MINS

4 large Tomatoes
3×15 ml spoons/3 tablespoons Fresh
    White Breadcrumbs
50 g/2 oz Finely chopped Ham
1×15 ml spoon/1 tablespoon Finely
    Chopped Parsley or Chives
13 g/½ oz Butter, melted
Salt and Pepper to taste
Garnish—parsley

METHOD
□ Cut tops off the tomatoes and keep
    for lids.
□ Scoop out the centre and mix with
    the rest of the ingredients.
    Season to taste.
□ Pile back into the tomatoes and put
    lid on each.
□ Place in a lightly buttered suitable
    container and cook for 2½ minutes
    on HIGH.
□ Garnish with parsley.

HOT SPICY GRAPEFRUIT
COOKING TIME 4 MINS

2 large Grapefruits
4×15 ml spoons/4 tablespoons Soft Brown
    Sugar
Little Butter
2×15 ml spoons/2 tablespoons Sherry
1×2.5 ml spoon/½ teaspoon ground
    cinnamon

METHOD
□ Cut grapefruit in half, remove any
    pips and loosen the segments.
□ Mix the remaining ingredients together
    and spread on top of the grapefruit.
    Dot each grapefruit with a little butter.
□ Cook on HIGH for 4 minutes, and
    serve immediately.

CHICKEN AND MUSHROOM VOL-AU-VENTS
COOKING TIME 4 MINS

25 g/1 oz Butter/Margarine
25 g/1 oz Plain Flour
150 ml/¼ pint Milk
175 g/6 oz Cooked Chicken
50 g/2 oz Chopped Mushrooms
1×5 ml spoon/1 teaspoon Oil
Salt and Pepper to taste
8 Small Pre-Baked Vol-Au-Vent Cases

METHOD
□ To make sauce, melt the butter on
    HIGH for 1 minute.
□ Add the flour and gradually whisk in
    milk.
□ Cook for 3 minutes on HIGH whisking
    after every minute to prevent lumps.
□ Dice the chicken.
□ Cook the mushrooms with oil for
    1 minute on HIGH.
□ Add the chicken and mushrooms to
    the sauce and mix thoroughly.
    Season to taste.
□ Spoon equal amounts of the chicken
    and mushroom mixture into the Vol-
    Au-Vent cases. Top with pastry lids.
□ The Vol-Au-Vents can be served hot
    or cold. Cook for 3 minutes if wanted
    hot.

HAM AND MUSHROOM VOL-AU-VENTS
Follow recipe for Chicken and Mushroom
Vol-Au-Vents, substitute 125 g/4 oz coarsley
chopped ham instead of chicken.

PRAWN VOL-AU-VENTS
Follow recipe and method for chicken and
mushroom Vol-Au-Vents. Instead of Chicken
and Mushroom use 125 g/4 oz peeled
prawns and 2×5 ml spoon/2 teaspoons of
lemon juice.

Hot Spicy Grapefruit ➜

CHICKEN LIVER PATE
COOKING TIME 8½ MINS
15g/½oz Butter
1 Small Onion, peeled and finely chopped
1 Garlic Clove, crushed
1×5ml spoon/1 teaspoon dried thyme
250g/8oz Chicken Livers, cleaned and
   chopped
2×15ml spoon/2 tablespoons Brandy or
Sherry
Salt & Freshly ground black pepper

METHOD
☐ Melt the butter for 30 seconds on
   HIGH.
☐ Add the onion garlic and thyme and
   cook on HIGH for 3 minutes.
☐ Add the chicken liver and cook on
   HIGH for 5 minutes, stirring frequently.
☐ Leave to cool slightly, then mince or
   puree in an electric blender until
   smooth.
☐ Work in brandy or sherry and season
   to taste.
☐ Press into a pate dish and refrigerate
   before serving with melba toast.

KIPPER PATE
COOKING TIME 4 MINS
250g/8oz Kipper Fillets
50g/2oz Butter
2×15ml spoon/2 tablespoons of cream
Black Pepper
1×15ml spoon/1 tablespoons Lemon Juice

METHOD
☐ Place the Kipper Fillets in a container,
   cook covered on HIGH for 3 minutes.
   Melt the butter on HIGH for 1 minute.
☐ Mince or blend the kippers and mix
   with half the melted butter. Then add
   the cream, black pepper and lemon
   juice. Beat the mixture until smooth.
☐ Turn onto a small pate dish and
   smooth the top. Cover with the
   remaining butter and chill.
   Serve with Melba toast or a salad.

CHEESE SOUFFLE
COOKING TIME 17½ MINS
25g/1oz Butter
25g/1oz Plain Flour
150ml/¼ pint Milk
Salt and pepper
2 Egg Yolks
2 Egg Whites
50g/2oz Grated Cheddar Cheese
1×2.5ml spoon/½ teaspoon dry mustard

METHOD
☐ Grease a 12.5cm–15cm (5-6 inch)
   Souffle dish.
☐ Put butter in a large bowl and cook
   on HIGH for 30 seconds.
☐ Add the flour and gradually add the
   milk. Cook on HIGH for 3 minutes,
   stirring at the end of every minute.
   Season and allow to cool.
☐ Stir in the egg yolks and cheese.
☐ Whisk egg whites until they form
   soft peaks. Carefully fold egg whites
   into sauce using a cutting and folding
   action.
☐ Pour into prepared dish and cook on
   ROAST for 14-15 minutes. Serve
   immediately.

FROM MIDDAY TO MIDNIGHT

Microwaves perform at their very best with sandwiches, hot drinks, soups, and chowders. For a quick pick-me-up all you need is a minute or two and a mug full of water for a cup of instant soup, or coffee. And, if you like to make soups from scratch without those endless hours of simmering and hovering that are required by conventional cooking, follow these microwave recipes.

Rise and shine with breakfast cocoa and wind down your day with after-dinner coffee swiftly and easily made in your microwave oven. What a convenience for coffee lovers! No more of that bitter mess when coffee is kept warm for more than 15 minutes in the conventional way. Brew your coffee as you normally do and pour what you want to drink now. Refrigerate the rest. Then, throughout the day, pour single cups as you wish from the refrigerated pot. Heat for 1½ to 2 minutes on HIGH and savour the taste of truly fresh coffee.

Converting Your Own Soup and Hot Drink Recipes

Soups and hot drinks convert well and easily to the microwave method. Find a recipe here with the approximate density and volume of the family favorite or the new conventional recipe you want to try. You may have to alter an ingredient or two: for example, dried bean soups such as split pea and navy bean do not obtain the best results in microwave cooking. However, canned, precooked navy beans, kidney beans, and packaged dry soup mixes are perfect substitutes for dried beans and peas. The tips below will help you obtain excellent results with your own recipes:

☐ Be careful with milk-based liquids or 2- or 3-quart quantities, which can boil over quickly. Always select a large enough microproof container to prevent any boiling over, and fill individual cups no more than two-thirds full.
☐ Soup is cooked covered. Use microproof casserole lids, or plastic wrap.
☐ Soup with uncooked meat and chicken needs slower simmering. Start cooking on HIGH and finish cooking on simmer. Generally, use reheat for soups containing cooked meats and/or vegetables.
☐ Cooking time varies with the volume of liquid and density of food in soup.
☐ Remember that the microwave's brief cooking time results in less evaporation of liquid than stovetop simmering.
☐ Start with one-quarter the time recommended in a conventional recipe and adjust as needed to complete cooking.

COOKING GUIDE— HOT DRINKS

Liquid	Cook Control Setting	6-ounce Cup	Time (in minutes)	8-ounce Cup	Time (in minutes)	Special Notes
Water	HIGH	1	1 to 1¼	1	1½ to 2	For instant coffee, soup, tea, etc.
		2	1¾ to 2	2	3 to 3¼	
Milk	70 (roast)	1	2½	1	2¾ to 3	For cocoa, etc.
		2	2¾ to 3	2	3¼ to 3½	
Reheating coffee	HIGH	1	1 to 1½	1	1¼ to 1½	
		2	2 to 2¼	2	2 to 2½	

COOKING GUIDE—CANNED SOUPS

Soup	Amount	Cook Control Setting	Time (in minutes)	Special Notes
Broth	10¾ oz.	Reheat	3½-4	Use 1½-quart casserole
Cream Style:	10¾ oz.	Reheat	5-6	Use 1½-quart casserole
Tomato	26 oz.	Reheat	8-10	Use 2-quart casserole
Bean, Pea, or Mushroom	10¾ oz.	Roast	7-8	Use 1½-quart casserole
Undiluted chunk-style vegetable:	10¾ oz.	Reheat	2½-4	Use 1-quart casserole
	19 oz.	Reheat	5-7	Use 1½-quart casserole

COOKING GUIDE—QUICK SOUPS

Soup	Number of Packets	Cook Control Setting	Time (in minutes)	Special Notes
Instant soup 1¼-ounce Packet	1	HIGH	2-2½	Use 2/3 cup water in 8-ounce mug.
	2	HIGH	3-3½	Use 2/3 cup water per 8-ounce mug.
	4	HIGH	6-7	Use 2/3 cup water per 8-ounce mug.
Soup mix 2¾-ounce Packet	1	HIGH	8-10	Use 4 cups water in 2-quart casserole.

Converting Your Own Sandwich Recipes

The enormous variety of sandwich combinations you can heat in your microwave oven will tickle your imagination and they are so easy to do. Combine meat and cheeses, eggs, salads, and vegetables; make elegant tea sandwiches; and, of course, you'll want to cook the old standbys, hot dogs and hamburgers. Sandwiches heat in seconds, so be careful not to overcook—the bread can become tough and chewy. Heat breads until warm, not hot, and cheese just until it begins to melt. You can warm meat sandwiches, filled only with several thin slices of meat per sandwich, on HIGH as follows:

    1 sandwich   45 to 50 seconds
    2 sandwiches 1 to 1½ minutes
    4 sandwiches 2 to 2½ minutes

Follow these tips when adapting or creating your own sandwiches:

☐ The best breads to use for warmed sandwiches are day-old, full-bodied breads such as rye and whole wheat, and breads rich in eggs and shortening, like French or Italian and other white breads.

☐ Heat sandwiches on paper napkins, paper towels, or paper plates to absorb the steam and prevent sogginess. Cover with a paper towel to prevent splattering. More simply, you can wrap each sandwich in a paper towel. Remove wrapping immediately after warming.

☐ Thin slices of meat heat more quickly and taste better than one thick slice. The slower-cooking thick slice often causes bread to overcook before meat is hot.

☐ Moist fillings, such as that in a barbecued beef sandwich, should generally be heated separately from the rolls, to prevent sogginess.

☐ The browning dish can be used to enhance your grilled cheese, or bacon sandwich. Brown the buttered outer side of bread before inserting filling.

CREAM OF LETTUCE SOUP
COOKING TIME 20 MINS
1 Medium Onion, peeled
1 Medium Potato, peeled
25 g/1 oz Butter
1 Large Lettuce, washed and shredded
450 ml/¾ pint Milk
300 ml/½ pint Chicken Stock
1×15 ml spoon/1 tablespoon White Wine
Few drops of Green Colouring
4×15 ml spoon/4 tablespoons Double Cream
Salt and Pepper

METHOD
☐ Dice onion and potato.
☐ Put butter, onions, potatoes, and lettuce in a large bowl and cook covered on HIGH for 12 minutes.
☐ Add milk, stock, wine and seasoning and heat on HIGH for 5 minutes.
☐ Pass through a sieve or electric blender and return to bowl.
☐ Season again if desired and also add green colouring if desired.
☐ Cook uncovered on HIGH for a further 3 minutes.
☐ Ladle in warm soup bowls and whirl on a tablespoon of cream.

BORSCHT
COOKING TIME 20 MINS
1 Large Carrot
2 Onions
4 Medium Cooked Beetroots
150 ml/¼ pint Water
600 ml/1 pint Beef Stock
125 g/4 oz White Cabbage, finely shredded
1×15 ml spoon/1 tablespoon Lemon Juice
Salt and Pepper to taste
Soured Cream

METHOD
☐ Peel and finely grate, carrot, onions and beetroot.
☐ Put into a large bowl with water and cook on HIGH for 5 minutes until boiling.
☐ Cover and cook on ROAST for 5 minutes. Add stock, cabbage, lemon juice and seasoning and cook covered on HIGH for a further 10 minutes. Ladle into individual bowls and serve with soured cream.

POTATO SOUP
COOKING TIME 20 MINS
37 g/1½ oz Butter
500 g/1 lb Potatoes, peeled and diced
1 Large Onion
450 ml/¾ pint Water
450 ml/¾ pint Milk
1×level 5 ml spoon/1 level teaspoon salt
Black Pepper
Chopped Chives
3×15 ml spoon/3 tablespoons Double Cream

METHOD
☐ Place butter, potatoes and onion in a large bowl and cook covered on HIGH for 10 minutes until soft.
☐ Add water, milk and seasoning and cook covered on HIGH until boiling.
☐ Ladle into soup bowls. Serve garnished with chopped chives and double cream.

VEGETABLE SOUP
COOKING TIME 27 MINS
50 g/2 oz Butter
2 Onions, peeled and chopped
2 Celery Stalks, chopped
500 g/1 lb Carrots, peeled and diced
1 Small Turnip, peeled and diced
1 Leek, shredded
25 g/1 oz Flour
900 ml/1½ pints Chicken Stock
2×5 ml spoon/2 teaspoons Salt

METHOD
☐ Put the butter and vegetables in a large bowl and cook uncovered on HIGH for 20 minutes.
☐ Stir in the flour and cook for a further 2 minutes on HIGH.
☐ Add stock and salt and cook uncovered on HIGH for a further 5 minutes. Pour into individual dishes.

VICHYSSOISE

COOKING TIME 18 MINS
2 Medium Leeks, sliced
1 Onion, chopped
50 g/2 oz Butter
2 Medium Potatoes
600 ml/1 pint Chicken Stock
1×5 ml spoon/1 teaspoon Salt
Black Pepper
Mace to taste
300 ml/½ pint Double Cream
Chopped Chives

METHOD
☐ Prepare leeks and onion. Put in a large bowl with butter and cook covered on HIGH for 5 minutes. Do not allow to brown.
☐ Thinly slice potatoes and add to bowl with stock, salt, pepper and mace, keep covered.
☐ Bring to boil (HIGH for 6 minutes), and cook on ROAST for 7 minutes or until vegetables are tender.
☐ Put through a sieve or electric blender.
☐ Chill thoroughly and just before serving stir in cream with chopped chives.

FRENCH ONION SOUP
COOKING TIME 22 MINS
3 Onions, peeled and finely sliced
50 g/2 oz Butter
1×15 ml spoon/1 tablespoon Cornflour
1 litre/1¾ pints Beef Stock
2×5 ml spoon/2 teaspoons Dry Sherry
50 g/2 oz Cheddar Cheese, grated
4 slices French Bread each 2-5 cm/1 inch thick, toasted
Salt and Black Pepper

METHOD
☐ Place onions and butter in a large bowl. Cook covered on HIGH for 10 minutes.

☐ Blend the cornflour with a little of the stock and add to the remaining stock. Add to the onions and butter and season to taste. Continue cooking for a further 10 minutes on HIGH.
☐ Add the sherry and pour into individual bowls.
☐ Sprinkle cheese onto bread and float a slice on each serving.
☐ Reheat each bowl on HIGH for 30 seconds each.

CREAM OF MUSHROOM SOUP
COOKING TIME 12 MINS
1 Small Onion
125 g/4 oz Mushrooms, cleaned and sliced
25 g/1 oz Butter
2×15 ml spoon/1 tablespoon Cornflour
150 ml/¼ pint Milk
1×15 ml spoon/1 tablespoon Lemon Juice
Salt and Pepper
Parsley chopped to garnish

METHOD
☐ Place onions, mushrooms and butter in a large heatproof bowl and cook on HIGH for 1 minute.
☐ Mix cornflour with a little milk and add with remaining milk and all other ingredients except lemon juice and parsley and cook on HIGH for 5 minutes.
☐ Stir vigorously. Cook again on HIGH for 4 minutes.
☐ Pass through a sieve or electric blender until smooth and return to the bowl.
☐ Cook on HIGH until the soup reaches boiling point (about 2 minutes). Stir in lemon juice. Pour into individual bowls and serve sprinkled with chopped parsley.

Vichyssoise ➡

TOMATO SOUP
COOKING TIME 13 MINS
37 g/1½ oz Butter
1 Onion, peeled and chopped
750 g/1½ lb Tomatoes, skinned and roughly
  chopped
25 g/1 oz Flour
600 ml/1 pint Chicken Stock
1×5 ml speen/1 teaspoon Dried Basil
1×5 ml spoon/1 teaspoon Worcester
Sauce
1×15 ml spoon/1 tablespoon Sherry
4×15 ml spoons/4 tablespoons Tomato Puree
1 Bay Leaf
Salt and Black Pepper

METHOD
☐ Put the butter and onion in a large
  bowl and cook on HIGH for 5 minutes.
☐ Add the tomatoes and cook on HIGH
  for a further 2 minutes.
☐ Stir in the flour and cook for a further
  2 minutes on HIGH.
☐ Gradually add the stock, basil,
  worcester sauce, tomato puree, bay
  leaf and seasonings. Cook uncovered
  on HIGH for 4 minutes.
☐ Remove bay leaf. Pass soup through
  a sieve or blender, then return to the
  bowl, and cook on HIGH until the
  soup is boiling.
  Serve with croutons.

COCOA
COOKING TIME 3 MINS
300 ml/½ pint Milk
2×5 ml spoon/2 teaspoons Cocoa

METHOD
☐ Combine milk and cocoa in a cup or
  mug.
☐ Cook for 3 minutes on HIGH.

HOT WINE PUNCH
COOKING TIME 7 MINS
75 g/3 oz Sugar
2 Sticks cinnamon
1 Lemon, sliced
12 Cloves
600 ml/1 pint Burgundy
300 ml/½ pint Water

METHOD
☐ Combine sugar, cinnamon, lemon
  and cloves with the water in a heatproof dish.
☐ Heat on HIGH for 2 minutes. Add
  burgundy, heat again for 5 minutes
  on HIGH.
☐ Strain and decorate with a twist of
  peeled orange or lemon peel in each
  glass.

HOT ALE PUNCH
COOKING TIME 7 MINS
600 ml/1 pint Beer
120 ml/4 fl. oz. Rum
120 ml/4 fl. oz. Gin
120 ml/4 fl. oz. Whisky
1 Lemon, sliced
Pinch Nutmeg
Pinch Cinnamon
Few Cloves
500 ml/1 pint Boiling Water
Sugar to taste

METHOD
☐ Put all spirits, beer, lemon and spices
  in a heatproof dish and heat on HIGH
  for 7 minutes.
☐ Add boiling water and sugar to taste.
☐ Decorate with a few slices of
  lemon peel.

LEMONADE
COOKING TIME 2½ MINS
Rind of 2 Lemons
Rind of 1 Orange
300 ml/½ pint Water
Juice of 4 Lemons
Juice of 2 Oranges
Sugar to taste

METHOD
☐ Put water in a heatproof dish and
  heat for 2½ minutes on HIGH until
  boiling.
☐ Pour over rinds and juice.
☐ Add sugar to taste.

Tomato Soup ➜

ICED TEA
COOKING TIME 5 MINS
3×15 ml spoon/3 tablespoons tea
4×15 ml spoon/4 tablespoons Sugar
Ice Cubes

METHOD
- ☐ Heat 600 ml/1 pint water for 5 minutes on HIGH.
- ☐ Add tea
- ☐ When desired strength is obtained, add sugar and stir.
- ☐ Serve over ice in tall glasses.

LEMON TEA
COOKING TIME 5 MINS
3×15 ml spoon/3 tablespoons Tea
Lemon Slices

METHOD
- ☐ Heat 600 ml/1 pint water on HIGH for 5 minutes.
- ☐ Add tea. Stir.
- ☐ Serve in tall glasses with a slice of lemon floating on top.

TEA WITH TEA BAGS
COOKING TIME 5 MINS
4 Tea Bags

METHOD
- ☐ Heat 600 ml/1 pint Water for 5 minutes on HIGH.
- ☐ Add tea bags. Remove when desired, strength is obtained.

INSTANT TEA
COOKING TIME 5 MINS
Tea to taste

METHOD
- ☐ Mix tea with 600 ml/1 pint water, and heat on HIGH for 5 minutes.

COFFEE
COOKING TIME 5 MINS
5×5 ml spoon/5 teaspoons instant coffee
Milk

METHOD
- ☐ Combine coffee, milk and 600 ml/1 1 pint water in a jug.
- ☐ Heat on HIGH for 5 minutes.

IRISH COFFEE
COOKING TIME 5 MINS
5×5 ml spoon/5 teaspoons instant coffee
125 ml/¼ pint Double Cream
Irish Whisky

METHOD
- ☐ Heat 600 ml/1 pint water on HIGH for 5 minutes. Add coffee.
- ☐ Put a tot of whisky in wine glasses, pour on coffee until about ¼ inch from top of glass.
- ☐ If sugar is desired, add to coffee and stir.
- ☐ Pour on cream over the back of a spoon.

NOTE:
Any spirits or liqueurs can be used instead of whisky depending on personal preference.

RING THE DINNER BELL FOR MEAT

Cooking meat in the microwave oven offers tremendous advantages over the conventional range. For juiciness and flavour, the microwave method excels. It also stretches your meat by reducing shrinkage. And you can defrost, cook, and reheat in minutes while your kitchen remains cool and comfortable.

If some of your guests or family prefer beef rare and others well done, the microwave oven solves the problem. After the roast is carved, a few seconds in the microwave oven will bring slices of rare roast to medium or well done.

In addition, meat for the barbecue is enhanced by precooking in the microwave. You get that wonderful charcoal flavour without the long watchful cooking that often results in burned or blackened meat. Microwave roasting methods are similar to dry roasting in your conventional oven. This means that the better, tender cuts of meat are recommended for best results. Less tender cuts should be marinated or tenderized and cooked at low power settings. As in conventional cooking, they are braised or stewed to achieve tenderness.

Meatloaf may be cooked in a loaf, but a ring mould is best. You can make your own ring mould by using a small straight-sided glass in baking dish (above). Food arrangement for microwave cooking is illustrated with lamb chops: the narrow bony end is placed toward the centre of the dish (above right).

Some people believe that meat does not brown in microwave ovens. Wrong! Any meat that cooks more than 10 minutes will brown in your microwave oven. True, individual steaks, chops, ground meat patties, and thin cuts of meat that cook quickly will brown best with a microproof browning dish.

Using the browning dish for Cheeseburgers

Converting Your Recipes

Charts on the following pages outline microwave thawing and cooking times for the standard cuts of meat. For converting casseroles, meatloaf, meat in sauces, and recipes that call for less tender cuts of meat, you're sure to find a similar recipe here to guide your own creations. Adapt your conventional recipes by matching ingredients and methods as closely as possible. Experiment as much as you like. Here are some helpful hints:

☐ For best results, cook evenly shaped, boned, rolled, and tied small roasts.
☐ Recipe times here presume meat is at refrigerator temperature. If your meal requires lengthy preparation, during which the meat may reach room temperature, reduce cooking times.
☐ Baste, marinate, or season meat just as you would for conventional cooking. However, avoid salting the surface before or during cooking, since salt tends to draw liquids from foods.
☐ Use a tight cover and a defrost or simmer setting for the less tender cuts of meat such as chuck, bottom round, brisket, and stewing meat cooked in liquid.
☐ Check dishes that use relatively long cooking times to be sure liquid has not evaporated. Add liquid as necessary.
☐ Enhance the colour and flavour of ground beef patties, steaks, meatloaf, and roasts by using one of the following: powdered brown gravy mix; a liquid browning agent; Worcestershire, soy sauce or steak sauce; paprika; cooked bacon; tomato sauce; or dehydrated onion soup mix.
☐ Most ground beef recipes call for lean meat. If you are using regular ground beef, drain fat before adding sauce ingredients.
☐ Large cuts not usually cooked on the charcoal grill, such as ham, leg of lamb, pork roast, turkey, and whole chicken, may be partially cooked in the microwave oven and finished on the grill for a lovely charcoal flavour and a browned crispness. It's also a great time saver for spareribs.

Using the Defrosting Guide

1. You may defrost meat within its original paper or plastic wrappings. Remove all metal rings, wire twist ties, and all foil wrapping.
2. Place meat in microproof dish.
3. Defrost in the microwave oven only as long as necessary, since standing time will complete the thawing process. Separate items like chops, bacon slices, and frankfurters into pieces as soon as possible. If separated pieces are not thawed, distribute them evenly in oven and continue defrosting.
4. Slightly increase the time for weights larger than on the chart. Do not double.
5. If you do not plan immediate cooking, follow the guide for only one-half to three quarters of recommended time. Place meat in refrigerator to continue defrosting until needed.

DEFROSTING GUIDE—MEAT

Meat	Amount	Cook Control Setting	Time (in minutes per pound)	Standing Time (in minutes)	Special Notes
Minced	1-lb.	Defrost	5-6	5	Turn over once. Remove thawed portions with fork. Return remainder. Freeze in doughnut shape. Depress center when freezing. Defrost on plate.
	2-lbs.	Defrost		5	
	¼-lb. patty	Defrost	1 per patty	2	
Pot roast, chuck	under 4 lbs.	Defrost	3-5	10	Turn over once.
	over 4 lbs.	Roast	3-5	10	Turn over once.
Rib roast, rolled	3 to 4 lbs.	Defrost	6-8	30-45	Turn over once.
	6 to 8 lbs.	Roast	6-8	90	Turn over twice.
Rib roast, bone in		Roast	5-6	45-90	Turn over twice.
Rump roast	3 to 4 lbs.	Defrost	3-5	30	Turn over once.
	6 to 7 lbs.	Roast	3-5	45	Turn over twice.
Round steak		Defrost	4-5	5-10	Turn over once.
Flank steak		Defrost	4-5	5-10	Turn over once.
Sirloin steak	½" thick	Defrost	4-5	5-10	Turn over once.
Tenderloin		Defrost	5-6	10	Turn over once.
Steaks	2 or 3 2 to 3 lbs.	Defrost	4-5	8-10	Turn over once.
Stew beef	2 lbs.	Defrost	3-5	8-10	Turn over once. Separate.
Lamb					
Cubed for stew		Defrost	7-8	5	Turn over once. Separate.
Ground lamb	under 4 lbs.	Defrost	3-5	30-45	Turn over once.
	over 4 lbs.	Roast	3-5	30-45	Turn over twice.
Chops	1" thick	Defrost	5-8	15	Turn over twice.
Leg	5-8 lbs.	Defrost	4-5	15-20	Turn over twice.
Pork					
Chops	½"	Defrost	4-6	5-10	Separate chops halfway
	1"	Defrost	5-7	10	through defrosting time.
Spareribs, country-style ribs		Defrost	5-7	10	Turn over once.
Roast	under 4 lbs.	Defrost	4-5	30-45	Turn over once.
	over 4 lbs.	Roast	4-5	30-45	Turn over twice.
Bacon	1-lb.	Defrost	2-3	3-5	Defrost until strips separate.
Sausage, bulk	1-lb.	Defrost	2-3	3-5	Turn over once. Remove thawed portions with fork. Return remainder
Sausage links	1 lb.	Defrost	3-5	4-6	Turn over once. Defrost until pieces can be separated.
Hot dogs		defrost	5-6	5	
Veal					
Roast	3 to 4 lbs.	Defrost	5-7	30	Turn over once.
	6 to 7 lbs.	Roast	5-7	90	Turn over twice.
Chops	½" thick	Defrost	4-6	20	Turn over once. Separate chops and continue defrosting.
Variety Meat					
Liver		Defrost	5-6	10	Turn over once.
Tongue		Defrost	7-8	10	Turn over once.

Using the Cooking Guide

1. Meat should be completely thawed before cooking.
2. Place meat fat side down, on microwave roasting rack set in glass baking dish. An inverted microproof saucer may be used if you do not have a roasting rack.
3. Meat may be covered lightly to stop splatters.
4. Unless otherwise noted, times given for steaks and patties will give medium cooking.
5. Minced beef to be used for cas-

seroles should be cooked briefly first; crumble it into a microproof dish and cook covered with a paper towel. Then drain off any fat and add meat to casserole.
6. During standing time, the internal temperature of roasts will rise approximately 8°C/15°F. Hence, standing time is considered an essential part of the time required to complete cooking.
7. Cutlets and chops that are breaded are cooked at the same time and cook control setting as shown on chart.

COOKING GUIDE—MEAT

Meat	Amount	First Cook Control Setting And Time	Second Cook Control Setting And Time	Standing Time (in minutes)	Special Notes
Beef Minced beef	Bulk	HIGH 2½ minutes per pound	Stir. HIGH 2½ minutes per pound	5	Crumble in dish, cook covered.
Minced beef patties, 4 oz., ½" thick	1	HIGH 1 minute	Turn over. HIGH 1-1½ minutes		Shallow baking dish.
	2	HIGH 1-1½ minutes	Turn over. HIGH 1-1½ minutes		shallow baking dish.
	4	HIGH 3 minutes	Turn over. HIGH 3-3½ minutes		Shallow baking dish.
Meatloaf	2 lbs.	HIGH 12-14 minutes		5-10	Glass loaf dish or glass ring mould.
Beef rib roast, boneless		HIGH Rare: 4-5 minutes per pound Medium: 5-6 minutes per pound Well: 6-7 minutes per pound	Turn over. (roast) 3-4 minutes per pound 5-6 minutes per pound 6-7 minutes per pound	10 10 10	Glass baking dish with microproof roasting rack.
Rib roast, bone in		HIGH Rare: 3-4 minutes per pound Medium: 4-5 minutes per pound Well: 5-6 minutes per pound	Turn over. (roast) 3-4 minutes per pound 3-5 minutes per pound 5-6 minutes per pound	10	Glass baking dish with microproof roasting rack.
Beef round, rump, or chuck, boneless		HIGH 5 minutes per pound	Turn over. (simmer) 20 minutes per pound	10-15	Casserole with tight cover. Requires liquid.
Beef brisket, boneless, fresh or corned	2½-3½ lbs.	HIGH 5 minutes per pound	Turn over. (simmer) 20 minutes per pound	10-15	4-quart casserole Dutch oven with tight cover. Water to cover.
Top round steak		HIGH 5 minutes per pound	Turn over. (simmer) 5 minutes per pound	10-15	Casserole with tight cover. Requires liquid.
Sirloin steak	¾ to 1" thick	HIGH 4½ minutes per pound	Drain dish and turn over. HIGH 2 minutes per pound	10-15	Shallow cooking dish or browning dish preheated 8 minutes on HIGH.

COOKING GUIDE—MEAT

Meat	Amount	First Cook Control Setting And Time	Second Cook Control Setting And Time	Standing Time (in minutes)	Special Notes
Minute steak or cube steak	4, 6 oz. steaks	HIGH 1-2 minutes	Drain dish and turn over. HIGH 1-2 minutes		Browning dish preheated on HIGH 8 minutes.
Tenderloin	4, 8-oz. steaks	HIGH Rare: 5 minutes Med: 6 minutes Well: 9 minutes	Drain, turn steak, HIGH 1-2 minutes 2-3 minutes 2-3 minutes	10-15	Browning dish preheated on HIGH 8 minutes.
Rib eye or strip steak	1½ to 2 lbs.	HIGH Rare: 4 minutes Med: 5 minutes Well: 7 minutes	Drain, turn steak, HIGH ½-1 minutes 1-2 minutes 2-3 minutes	10-15	Browning dish preheated on HIGH 8 minutes.
Lamb Ground lamb patties	1-2 lbs.	HIGH 4 minutes	Turn over. HIGH 4-5 minutes		Browning dish preheated on HIGH 7 minutes.
Lamb chops	1-1½ lbs. 1" thick	HIGH 8 minutes	Turn over. HIGH 7-8 minutes		Browning dish preheated on HIGH 7 minutes.
Lamb leg or shoulder roast, bone in		70 (roast) Medium: 4-5 minutes per pound Well: 5-6 minute per pound	Cover end of leg bone with foil. Turn over. 70 (roast) Medium: 4-5 minutes per pound Well: 5-6 minutes per pound	5 10	12×7-inch dish with microproof roasting rack.
Lamb roast, boneless		(Roast) 5-6 minutes per pound	Turn over. (roast) 5-6 minutes per pound	10	12×7-inch dish with microproof roasting rack.
Veal: Shoulder or rump roast, boneless	2-5 lbs.	(Roast) 9 minutes per pound	Turn over. (roast) 9-10 minutes per pound	10	12×7-inch dish with microproof roasting rack.
Veal cutlets or loin chops	½" thick	HIGH 2 minutes per pound	Turn over. HIGH 2-3½ minutes per pound		Browning dish preheated on HIGH 7-10 minutes.
Pork: Pork chops	½" thick	HIGH 6 minutes per pound	Turn over. HIGH 5-6 minutes per pound		Browning dish preheated on HIGH 7 minutes
Spareribs		(Roast) 6-7 minutes per pound	Turn over. (roast) 6-7 minutes per pound	10	12×7-inch dish with microproof roasting rack.
Pork loin roast, boneless	3-5 lbs.	HIGH 6 minutes per pound	Turn over. (roast) 5-6 minutes per pound	10	12×7-inch dish with microproof roasting rack.
Pork loin, centre cut	4-5 lbs.	HIGH 5-6 minutes per pound	Turn over. 4-5 minutes per pound	10	13×9-inch dish with microproof roasting rack.
Ham, boneless, precooked		(Roast) 5-7 minutes per pound	Turn over. (roast) 5-7 minutes per pound	10	12×7-inch dish with microproof roasting rack.
Centre cut ham slice	1-1½ lbs.	(Roast) 5 minutes per pound	Turn over. (roast) 5-6 minutes per pound	10	12×7-inch baking dish.
Smoked ham shank		(Roast) 4-5 minutes per pound	Turn over. (roast) 4-5 minutes per pound	10	12×7-inch dish with microproof roasting rack.

COOKING GUIDE—MEAT

Meat	Amount	First Cook Control Setting And Time	Second Cook Control Setting And Time	Standing Time (in minutes)	Special Notes
Canned ham	3 lbs.	(Roast) 5-6 minutes per pound	(Roast) 5-6 minutes per pound	10	12×7-inch dish with microproof roasting rack.
	5 lbs.	70 (roast) 4-5 minutes per pound	Turn over. (roast) 4-5 minutes per pound	10	12×7-inch dish with microproof roasting rack.
Sausage patties	12-oz.	HIGH 2 minutes	Turn over. HIGH 1½-2 minutes per pound		Browning dish preheated on HIGH 7 minutes
Sausage	16 oz.	HIGH 3 minutes	Stir. HIGH 1-2 minutes		Crumble into 1½-quart dish, covered.
Pork sausage links	½ lb.	Pierce casing HIGH 1 minute	Turn over. HIGH 1-1½ minutes		Browning dish preheated on HIGH 7 minutes
	1 lb.	HIGH 2 minutes	HIGH 1½-2 minutes		
Bratwurst, precooked		Pierce casing (roast) 5 minutes per pound	Rearrange, (roast) 4-5 minutes per pound		Casserole.
Polish sausage, knockwurst, ring bologna		Pierce casing 80 (reheat) 2-2½ minutes per pound	Rearrange (reheat) 2-2½ minutes per pound		Casserole.
Hot dogs	1	(Reheat) 25-30 seconds			Shallow dish.
	2	80 (reheat) 25-40 seconds			Shallow dish.
	4	80 (reheat) 50-55 seconds			Shallow dish.
Bacon 2 slices		HIGH 1½-2 minutes			Dish: slices between paper towels
4 slices		HIGH 3-4 minutes			Dish: slices between paper towels
6 slices		HIGH 4½-6 minutes			Roasting rack, slices covered with paper towels
8 slices		HIGH 5-6 minutes			Roasting rack, slices covered with paper towels

Special Tips about Bacon

☐ Cook bacon on a paper-lined plate, and cover with paper towels to prevent splatters and absorb drippings.

☐ To reserve drippings, cook bacon on a meat rack in a baking dish or on a microwave bacon rack. Bacon can also be cooked, in slices or cut up, in a casserole and removed if necessary with a slotted spoon.

☐ For bacon that is soft rather than crisp, cook at the minimum timing.

☐ Bacon varies in quality. The thickness and amount of sugar and salt used in curing will affect browning and timing. Cook thicker slices a bit longer than the chart indicates. You will also find that sweeter bacon cooks more quickly.

☐ Sugar in bacon causes brown spots to appear on the paper towels. If the bacon tends to stick a bit to the towel, it is due to an extra high amount of sugar.

COOKING/DEFROSTING GUIDE— CONVENIENCE BEEF

Food	Amount	Cook Control Setting	Time (in minutes)	Special Notes
Barbecued beef, chili, stew, hash, meatballs, etc.	16 oz. or less (cans)	Reheat	3-5	Remove from cans to microproof plate or casserole, cover. Stir halfway through cooking time.
Stuffed peppers, cabbage rolls, chow mein, etc.	16-32 oz. (cans)	Reheat	5-9	
Barbecued beef, chili, stew, corned beef hash, meatballs, patties in sauce, gravy	8-16 oz. package (frozen)	HIGH	5-11	Remove from foil container to microproof casserole, cover. Slit plastic pouches.
Dry casserole mixes, cooked hamburger added	6½-8 oz. package	HIGH	18-22	Remove mix from package to 3-quart microproof casserole. Cover. Stir once.

TRADITIONAL BEEF STEW
COOKING TIME 70-80 MINS
1 kg/2 lb Stewing Steak, cubed
250 g/8 oz Mushrooms, sliced
300 ml/½ pint Beef Stock
3 celery stalks cut into pieces
3 Medium Carrots, peeled and cut into slices
2 Potatoes, peeled and cut into cubes
Bouquet Garni
25 g/1 oz Flour
Salt and Pepper

METHOD
☐ Put meat, mushrooms and stock into a casserole dish. Cook covered on DEFROST for 40 minutes.
☐ Add celery, carrots, potatoes, bouquet garni and seasoning and stir lightly. Mix flour to a paste with a little water. Stir into the stew. Add more stock if desired.
☐ Cook covered on DEFROST for 30-40 minutes until the vegetables are tender.
☐ Remove bouquet garni and stand for 5 minutes.

BEEF CASSEROLE
COOKING TIME 73 MINS
750 g/1½ lb Stewing Steak, cut into 1 inch cubes
3×15 ml spoon/3 tablespoons Oil
2 Leeks, sliced
2 Carrots, sliced very thinly
1 Onion, chopped
25 g/1 oz Flour
150 ml/¼ pint Beef Stock
425 g/14 oz Tin Tomatoes, chopped (397 g on tin)
Seasoning

METHOD
☐ Trim any excess fat off the meat, heat 2×15 ml spoon/2 tablespoons of oil in ovenproof dish. Add meat and cook for 8 minutes on DEFROST, until browned.
☐ Add the leeks and the carrots. Heat the remaining oil in a separate dish and fry the onions until soft, for approximately 4 minutes on HIGH. Add to the casserole dish.
☐ Combine the flour with a little of the stock and pour into the casserole with the rest of the stock.
☐ Heat for 56 minutes on DEFROST (covered), until thickened. Pour in tomatoes and add seasoning.
☐ Cook covered on HIGH for 5 minutes and serve.

BEEF BOURGIGNON
COOKING TIME 68 MINS

750 g/1½ lb Stewing Steak, cubed
25 g/1 oz Lard
175 g/6 oz Bacon, chopped
1×15 ml spoon/1 tablespoon flour
150 ml/¼ pint Red Wine
300 ml/½ pint Beef Stock
Bay Leaf
Parsley
Bouquet Garni
Seasoning

METHOD
☐ Preheat a browning skillet for 5 minutes or according to manufacturer's instructions.
☐ Melt fat in a browning skillet or ovenproof dish on HIGH for 30 seconds. Cook the bacon and steak for 5 minutes on HIGH until steak is brown on all sides.
☐ Put into a casserole dish. Add the flour to dish and cook on HIGH for 30 seconds.
☐ Add stock and wine and cook for 2 minutes on HIGH until boiling and thick. Stir in bay leaf, Bouquet Garni, parsley and seasoning.
☐ Pour over the meat and cook on SIMMER for 55 minutes.

BEEF AND TOMATO KEBABS
COOKING TIME 12 MINS

750 g/1½ lb Sirloin or rump steak, marinated   overnight.
8 Firm tomatoes, halved
1 Large green pepper, deseeded and cut into cubes.

FOR THE SAUCE OR MARINADE
2×15 ml spoon/2 tablespoons Soy Sauce
1×15 ml spoon/1 tablespoon Worcestershire Sauce
1×15 ml spoon/1 tablespoon Lemon Juice
2×15 ml spoon/2 tablespoons Tomato Ketchup
2×15 ml spoon/2 tablespoons Oil
Seasoning

METHOD
☐ Cut the meat into cubes. Mix all the ingredients for the marinade and add the meat to marinate and leave over night.
☐ Thread the meat, tomatoes and pepper alternately onto four skewers. Brush kebabs with any remaining sauce from marinade.
☐ Put kebabs in a suitable dish and cook on HIGH for 12 minutes, turning over half way through cooking.
☐ Serve on a bed of rice or with a salad.

CORDON BLEU VEAL
COOKING TIME 11 MINS

4×125 g/4×4 oz Slices veal escalope
125 g/4 oz Cooked ham, thinly sliced
2 Slices of Swiss Cheese
1 Egg, beaten
50 g/2 oz Dry breadcrumbs
4 Tablespoons Oil

METHOD
☐ Beat the veal to flatten, either with a mallet or rolling pin.
☐ Place a slice of ham and cheese onto each piece of veal and fold over completely enclosing the ham and cheese.
☐ Dip into the beaten egg and then dip into the breadcrumbs.
☐ Preheat a large browning skillet for 5 minutes. Add the oil quickly and then the veal. Cook on HIGH for 1 minute. Turn the veal over and microwave on HIGH for 5 minutes.
☐ Drain on absorbent paper and serve immediately, garnished with parsley and lemon wedges.

BEEF & GREEN PEPPERS
COOKING TIME 11-12 MINS
2×15ml spoon/2 tablespoons Oil
500g/1lb Sirloin Steak or Rump Steak
1 Onion, peeled and finely chopped
1 Large Green Pepper
1 Meat Extract cube (e.g. Oxo)
Salt & Pepper

METHOD
☐ Place the oil in a casserole dish.
☐ Cut the beef into thin strips and toss in the oil. Add the onion, salt and pepper.
☐ Cook, covered for 6 minutes on HIGH stirring once during cooking.
☐ Wash, deseed and cut the pepper into strips, add to the beef.
☐ Crumble the beef extract cube over the beef and peppers and cook, covered for 5-6 minutes on HIGH. Serve with rice or noodles.

SAVOURY MEATBALLS AND TOMATO SAUCE
COOKING TIME 12½ MINS
500g/1lb Minced Beef
50g/2oz Breadcrumbs
4×15ml spoon/4 tablespoons Milk
1 Small Onion, grated
1×5ml spoon/1 teaspoon Worcestershire Sauce
Seasoning
12g/½oz Butter

SAUCE
1×15ml spoon/1 tablespoon Cornflour
397g/14oz Can Tomatoes, sieved
Salt and Pepper
1×5ml spoon/1 teaspoon Mixed Herbs

METHOD
☐ Combine all ingredients except butter together.
☐ Divide mixture into 16 small meatballs. Melt butter on HIGH for 30 seconds in a microproof container.
☐ Arrange meatballs, in the dish a and cook on HIGH for 7 minutes. Make up the sauce.
☐ Blend cornflour with a little juice from the tomatoes. Add rest of juice and mixed herbs and cook for 5 minutes on HIGH until boiling.
☐ Stir occasionally until clear. Taste, and adjust seasoning. Pour over the meatballs and serve.

LIVER WITH ORANGE
COOKING TIME 13 MINS
475g/12oz Calves Liver, cut in thin slices
15g/½oz Seasoned Flour
25g/1oz Margarine or Butter
1 Onion, chopped
1 Clove Garlic, crushed
1×15ml spoon/1 tablespoon Parsley, chopped
Pinch Salt
4×15ml spoon/4 tablespoons Stock
2×15ml spoon/2 tablespoons Red Wine
1 Large Orange
Brown Sugar

METHOD
☐ Dip the liver in the seasoned flour. Melt half the butter in the preheated browning skillet or dish, and saute the liver quickly on both sides, on HIGH for 2 minutes. Remove.
☐ Put remaining butter or margarine into a dish and add onion and garlic. Cook on HIGH for 5 minutes.
☐ Add parsley, salt, stock and wine. Bring to boil by cooking on HIGH for 2 minutes.
☐ Pour over the liver and cook for 3 minutes on HIGH.
☐ Cut orange into thin slices and coat in the brown sugar.
☐ Place over liver and cook on HIGH for 1 minute. Serve straight away.

MINCED BEEF MEAT LOAF
COOKING TIME 20 MINS
500 g/1 lb Minced Beef
4×15 ml spoon/4 tablespoons Sage and
 Onion Stuffing Mix
1×15 ml spoon/1 tablespoon Worcestershire
 Sauce
1×15 ml spoon/1 tablespoon Tomato
 Ketchup
1 Onion, grated
1 Clove Garlic, crushed
Salt and Pepper
1 Egg, beaten

SAUCE
2×5 ml spoon/2 teaspoons Cornflour
400 g/14 oz Can Tomatoes
Salt and Pepper

METHOD
- ☐ Place all ingredients in a bowl and combine well. Spoon the contents into an oblong dish and press down well.
- ☐ Cook uncovered on HIGH for 15 minutes. Cover and leave to stand for 10 minutes.
- ☐ For the sauce, blend the cornflour with a little juice from the tomatoes in a dish.
- ☐ Add rest of the juice and tomatoes and cook for 5 minutes on HIGH, until boiling. Stir occasionally until clear.
- ☐ Taste and adjust the seasoning. Turn meat loaf out onto a dish and pour over tomato sauce.

BEEFBURGERS
COOKING TIME 2½-3½ MINS
250 g/8 oz Finely Minced Beef
1 Small Onion, peeled and grated
25 g/1 oz Fresh breadcrumbs
1 Egg size 5/small, beaten
Salt and pepper

METHOD
- ☐ Mix the minced beef, onion, salt, pepper and breadcrumbs together and bind with the beaten egg.
- ☐ Divide the mixture into 4 balls and then flatten them.
- ☐ Put the beefburgers onto a plate and cook on HIGH for 2½-3½ minutes.

NOTE:
For a crisper beefburger, preheat a browning skillet for 5 minutes. Place the beefburgers in the skillet and cook for 2½-3½ minutes turning over half way through cooking.

CHILI CON CARNE
COOKING TIME 24½ MINS
2×5 ml spoon/2 teaspoons Olive Oil
25 g/1 oz Butter
2 Medium Onions, Chopped
1 Clove Garlic, Finely Chopped
500 g/1 lb Minced Beef
397 g can/14 oz Can Tomatoes
1 Green Pepper, deseeded,
1×5 ml spoon/1 teaspoon Chili Powder
2×15 ml spoon/2 tablespoons Tomato Puree
1×2.5 ml spoon/½ level teaspoon Salt
425 g/15 oz Can Red Kidney Beans, 75 ml/⅛
Pint Water
2×15 ml spoon/2 tablespoons Cornflour
6×15 ml spoon/6 tablespoons Single Cream

METHOD
- ☐ Melt oil and butter in a large dish for 30 seconds on HIGH.
- ☐ Gently fry the onion and garlic in the fat for 3 minutes on HIGH.
- ☐ Add minced beef and cook uncovered for 4 minutes on HIGH until meat loses its red colour. Chop tomatoes and green pepper. Add to dish with remaining seasonings and kidney beans.
- ☐ Cover and cook for 15 minutes on ROAST.
- ☐ Combine cornflour with a little cold water and pour into dish. Stir, cook for another 2 minutes on HIGH.
- ☐ Before serving, stir in the cream.

SHEPHERDS PIE
COOKING TIME 31 MINS
500g/1 lb Minced Beef
25g/1 oz Butter
1×5ml spoon/1 teaspoon Oil
1 Onion, chopped
50g/2oz Mushrooms
25g/1 oz Flour
150ml/¼ pint Beef Stock
2×5ml spoon/2 teaspoons Tomato Puree
1 Small Bay Leaf
Parsley
1×5ml spoon/1 teaspoon Worcestershire
　　Sauce
Pinch of Mixed Herbs
Seasoning to taste
1000g/2lb Potatoes, peeled and cut into
　　small pieces.

METHOD
☐ Heat butter and oil in a dish and
cook onion and mushrooms on
HIGH for 2 minutes. Add flour and
cook for 1 minute.
☐ Put mince in a dish and cook on
HIGH for 3 minutes.
☐ Blend in stock gradually stirring all
the time until it thickens. Add puree,
bay leaf, parsley, Worcestershire
sauce, herbs and seasoning and
cook on ROAST for 15 minutes,
stirring once.
☐ Remove from oven and remove bay
leaf.
☐ Put potatoes in a dish with a little
salted water, cover and cook for
10 minutes on HIGH.
☐ Drain off water and mash until
smooth. Spoon over mince and
decorate with back of fork.
☐ Serve with fresh green vegetables.

STEAK AND KIDNEY PUDDING
SUET PASTRY
COOKING TIME 52 MINS
250g/8oz Self Raising Flour
1×5ml spoon/1 teaspoon salt
75g/3oz Shredded Beef Suet
150ml/¼ pint Water

FILLING
500g/1 lb Stewing Beef, trimmed and
cubed
300ml/½ pint Brown Stock
125g/4oz Ox Kidney, cleaned and chopped
Salt & Pepper

METHOD
☐ Put the beef and stock into a suitable
container. Season.
☐ Cook, covered for about 38 minutes
on DEFROST, until meat is just tender.
Then add the kidney and cook for a
further 5 minutes on ROAST.
☐ Meanwhile, make the pastry: Sift the
flour and salt into a mixing bowl.
☐ Stir in the shredded suet and mix in
the water gradually, to form a soft
dough. Knead lightly on a floured
surface.
☐ Roll into the shape of a 900ml/1½
pint pudding basin. Cut one quarter
of the round for the lid, and reserve.
☐ Grease the basin and fit the pastry
lining.
☐ Place the steak and kidney and gravy
into the basin.
☐ Roll the remaining pastry into a round,
large enough to form a lid for the
pudding basin. Wet the edges of the
pastry lid, place over the meat and
seal the edges.
☐ Cook, covered on HIGH for 9 minutes.
Leave to stand 5 minutes before
serving.

NOTE:
Mushrooms can be substituted for the kidney.

LANCASHIRE HOT POT
CONVENTIONAL COOKING TIME—
15-20 MINS. MICROWAVE COOKING
TIME—20 MINS

500g/1lb Potatoes, peeled and sliced into
  rings
25g/1oz Beef Dripping or Lard for Frying
750g/1lb 8oz Best End of Neck Lamb
  Chops
2 Lambs Kidneys, cleaned and chopped
Salt & Pepper
1 large onion peeled, and finely chopped
150ml/¼ pint Stock

METHOD
☐ Put half the potato rings in a layer on
the bottom of a deep Microwave
Casserole dish. Season well with salt
and pepper.
☐ Melt the beef dripping or lard in a
frying pan or hot browning dish.
☐ Add the chops and kidneys and
brown quickly on all sides.
☐ Lay the chops and kidney on top of
the potatoes, add the onion. Pour
over the stock.
☐ Put the remaining potatoes in a layer
on top. Cover and cook on ROAST
for 20 minutes.
☐ Remove cover and brown in a hot
oven for 15-20 minutes (400°F
200°C — Gas Mark 6).

PARTY GAMMON
COOKING TIME MICROWAVE 7-8
MINS PER ½KG/1LB CONVENTIONAL
COOKING TIME 30 MINS

1 Piece of Gammon 1.5 to 1.75kg/3lb—
  8oz -4lb after boning.
Cloves
75g/3oz Soft Brown Sugar
15g/½oz Melted Butter
2×15ml spoon/2 tablespoons clear Honey

METHOD
☐ Soak the Gammon overnight to
remove excess salt. Drain.
☐ Allow 7-8 minutes per ½kg/1lb on
HIGH in the microwave. If the joint is
narrower at one end, cover the narrow
part with foil to prevent overcooking
and remove halfway through cooking.

☐ Cook for half the cooking time and
then turn over.
☐ Leave to stand for 10-15 minutes.
Strip off skin, score fat into diamond
pattern.
☐ Press in a clove in each alternate
diamond.
☐ Place the Joint in a roasting tin.
☐ Combine the remaining ingredients
together and coat the fat with this
mixture.
☐ Cook in the centre of a hot oven
(190°C/375°F or Gas No. 5) for 30
minutes or until fat is golden brown.
Baste 3 or 4 times. Serve hot or cold.

SWEET AND SOUR PORK
COOKING TIME 35½ MINS

750g/1½lb Pork, cubed
Salt and Pepper
1½×5ml spoon/1½ teaspoons Ground
  Ginger
1×15ml spoon/1 tablespoons Oil
1 Small Onion, finely chopped
1 Green Pepper, de-seeded, chopped
2×15ml spoon/2 tablespoons Cornflour
3×15ml spoon/3 tablespoons Vinegar
2×5ml spoon/2 teaspoons Soy Sauce
1×5ml spoon/1 teaspoon Tomato Ketchup
1½×15ml spoon/1½ tablespoon brown
  sugar
150ml/¼ pint Chicken Stock
425g/16oz can Pineapple pieces,
  (454g on can)

METHOD
☐ Toss pork in the ground ginger, place
in a casserole dish and cook on
ROAST for 20 minutes. Put on one
side.
☐ Put oil, onion and green pepper in a
dish and cook for 2 minutes on
HIGH till softened.
☐ Drain the pineapple syrup into a heat
resistant bowl. Add stock, sugar,
vinegar, soy sauce, ketchup and
cornflour and stir well.
☐ Cook on HIGH for 3½ minutes,
stirring twice.
☐ Add the pineapple, onion and green
pepper and mix well.
☐ Pour over the pork and cook on
ROAST for 10 minutes.
☐ Serve immediately on a border of
boiled rice.

PORK CHOPS WITH CIDER
COOKING TIME 9½ MINS

4 Lean Chops
15g/½oz Butter
15g/½oz Flour
150ml/¼ pint Cider
75ml/⅛ pint Water
Salt and Pepper
1×5ml spoon/1 teaspoon Dried Sage
2×15ml spoon/2 tablespoons Fresh Cream
1 Onion, Chopped

METHOD

☐ Melt butter in a preheated browning skillet or oven proof dish for 30 seconds on HIGH. Fry chops together with onion for 2 minutes on each side on HIGH.
☐ Remove chops and place in a dish.
☐ Put onions in a dish, add flour to onions and cook for 1 minute on HIGH. Stir in cider, water, seasoning and sage.
☐ Pour over the chops and cook for 6 minutes on ROAST. Before serving pour the cream over the chops.

STUFFED PORK CHOPS
COOKING TIME 12 MINS

4×125g/4×4oz Pork Chops
2×5ml spoon/2 teaspoons gravy powder
50g/2oz Breadcrumbs
1 Eating Apple, peeled and chopped
2×15ml spoon/2 tablespoons grated onion
25g/1oz Butter, melted
Salt and pepper

METHOD

☐ Trim some of the fat from the pork chops.
☐ Sprinkle one side of each chop with gravy powder and place the chops coated side down in a large shallow dish.
☐ Mix the remaining ingredients together and season with salt and pepper to taste.
☐ Spread the stuffing over each pork chop. Cover and cook on HIGH for 12 minutes.

BARBECUED SPARE RIBS
COOKING TIME 20 MINS

450g/1lb Pork Spare Ribs
1 Onion, peeled and chopped
1×15ml spoon/1 tablespoon Cooking Oil
3×15ml spoon/3 tablespoons Soy Sauce
2×15ml spoon/2 tablespoons Lemon Juice
1×15ml spoon/1 tablespoon Sherry (optional)
150ml/¼ pint Beef Stock, made from ½ meat extract cube
2×15ml spoon/2 tablespoons Brown Sugar

METHOD

☐ Divide the spare ribs and place in a shallow container. Cook, covered on HIGH for 7 minutes. Drain off any fat.
☐ Place the onion and oil in another container and cook on HIGH for 2 minutes.
☐ Mix the remaining ingredients, with the onion and pour over the ribs.
☐ Cook on ROAST for 11 minutes.

GAMMON & PINEAPPLE
COOKING TIME 5 MINS

2×175g/2×6oz Slices of Gammon Steaks
1×227g/8oz Can of Pineapple Rings
1×15ml spoon/1 tablespoon Brown Sugar
Little Butter

METHOD

☐ Remove the rind and cut through the fat at 2.5cm/1 inch intervals with kitchen scissors to prevent the meat curling up during cooking.
☐ Arrange the gammon steaks in a large shallow dish and sprinkle with sugar, dot with butter and cook covered on HIGH for 4 minutes.
☐ Then place the drained pineapple rings on top and cook for a further 1 minute on HIGH.

YORKSHIRE DEVILLED KIDNEYS
COOKING TIME 17½ MINS
4 Pigs Kidneys
3×15 ml spoon/3 tablespoons Seasoned
  Flour
25 g/1 oz Butter,
Small Onion
150 ml/¼ pint Water
2×5 ml spoon/2 teaspoons Worcestershire
  sauce
2×5 ml spoon/2 teaspoons Tomato Puree
1×2.5 ml spoon/½ teaspoon English Made
  Mustard
Parsley, chopped
4 Slices Hot Toast
Seasoning

METHOD
☐ Skin and core kidneys and cut into
  small strips. Toss in the seasoned flour.
☐ Melt the butter in a dish for 30
  seconds on HIGH. Add the onion
  and cook for 2 minutes on HIGH.
☐ Add Kidney and remaining flour.
  Cook on ROAST for 5 minutes.
☐ Combine water with Worcestershire
  sauce, tomato puree, mustard and
  parsley. Pour into the dish. Cook on
  HIGH for 5 minutes until boiling and
  thick.
☐ Cook covered on ROAST for 5
  minutes. Serve with the hot toast.

LIVER CASSEROLE
COOKING TIME 17 MINS
500 g/1 lb Lambs Liver
37 g/1½ oz Seasoned Flour
50 g/2 oz Margarine
1 Onion, chopped
2 Rashers Bacon, chopped
125 g/4 oz Button Mushrooms, washed
150 ml/¼ pint Chicken Stock
150 ml/¼ pint Soured Cream
Chopped Chives

METHOD
☐ Cut liver into ½ inch strips and toss in
  the seasoned flour. Heat half the
  margarine 1 minute on HIGH in the
  preheated browning skillet or frying
  pan and fry the liver on HIGH for 2
  minutes until lightly browned.
☐ Remove, add remaining margarine
  and fry onion, bacon and mushrooms
  for 6 minutes on HIGH. Transfer to a
  casserole dish.
☐ Add stock to casserole dish, heat on
  HIGH for 2 minutes until boiling.
☐ Stir, add liver and cook for a further
  4 minutes on HIGH. Pour in the
  cream and reheat for 2 minutes.
☐ Serve with boiled rice and garnish
  with chopped chives.

LAMB CHOPS BOULANGERE
COOKING TIME 15 MINS
250 g/8 oz Cooked Potatoes
250 g/8 oz Cooked Carrots
4 Lamb Chump Chops
1 Small Onion peeled & Finely Chopped
15 g/½ oz Butter
Salt & Pepper

METHOD
☐ Slice the potatoes and carrots and
  arrange in a single layer in a shallow
  casserole dish.
☐ Place the chops on top of the
  vegetables and then cover with onions.
☐ Dot with the butter and sprinkle with
  salt and pepper.
☐ Cover, cook on HIGH for 15 minutes.

LAMB CHOPS WITH ROSEMARY
COOKING TIME 12-15 MINS
4 Large Lamb Chops
15 g/½ oz Butter/melted
Sprinkling of chopped rosemary
Garlic Powder or salt
Freshly ground black pepper

METHOD
☐ Place the lamb chops in a shallow dish.
☐ Brush with the melted butter. Sprinkle
  with the rosemary, garlic powder or
  salt and black pepper.
☐ Cook, covered on HIGH for 12-15
  minutes.

← *Stuffed Pork Chops*

CURRIED LAMB
COOKING TIME 38½ MINS
25g/1oz Butter
2 Small Onions, chopped
1 Clove Garlic, crushed
1×15ml spoon/1 tablespoon curry Powder
1×15ml spoon/1 tablespoon (level) Flour
2 Tomatoes, skinned and chopped
1 Bay Leaf
1×5ml spoon/1 tablespoon Cinnamon
25g/1oz Sultanas
4 Cloves
1 Large Cooking Apple, grated
1×15ml spoon/1 tablespoon Sweet Pickle
1×5ml spoon/1 teaspoon Salt
300ml/½ pint Beef Stock
1kg/2lb Middle Neck of Lamb cubed

METHOD
☐ Melt butter for 30 seconds on HIGH.
☐ Cook onion and garlic for 5 minutes on HIGH. Stir in curry powder, flour, tomatoes, bay leaf, cinnamon, sultanas, cloves, apples, sweet pickle and salt.
☐ Blend in stock. Add lamb and bring to boil by cooking for 5 minutes on HIGH.
☐ Switch to SIMMER and cook for 28 minutes.
☐ Remove bay leaf and cloves. Serve with boiled rice.

CROWN ROAST OF LAMB
COOKING TIME 51 MINS
50g/2oz Butter
1 Onion, chopped
Lemon Juice
Salt and Pepper
Garlic Powder
25g/3oz Packet of Sage and Onion Stuffing
1 Egg
2kg/4lb Crown Roast
Paper Frills

METHOD
☐ Put butter in a bowl and heat on HIGH for 1 minute, add onion and cook on HIGH for 5 minutes.
☐ Stir in lemon juice, salt and pepper, garlic powder and stuffing, made up as directed on packet but slightly stiff, and mix thoroughly. Bind mixture with beaten egg.
☐ Arrange roast on a suitable baking dish, and spoon mixture into centre. Cook uncovered on ROAST for 45 minutes.
☐ Cover crown roast with aluminium foil and leave to stand for 20-30 minutes.
☐ Top each bone with a paper frill.

NOTE:
If crown roast is a little too high for the oven, trim top of cutlets.

PRIME TIME POULTRY

Chicken, turkey, and duck, are especially juicy, tender, and tasty when cooked in a microwave oven. Because they require less attention than other meats, they are great favourites for microwave cooks on those days when too many things seem to be happening at once. Poultry turns out golden brown but not crisp. If you have crisp-skin lovers at your table, you can satisfy them by crisping the skin in a conventional oven at 230°C/450°F, after the microwave cooking. You can also avoid the frustrations of long barbecue cooking by partially cooking poultry in the microwave oven, then finishing it off on the charcoal grill. Try the tasty recipes suggested here and then adapt your own. You'll even want to experiment with new recipes when you discover how much easier it is to cook poultry in your microwave oven than in the conventional oven.

A browning sauce may be brushed on poultry before cooking if you prefer a more-browned appearance than the microwave normally provides (above left). The best arrangement for chicken parts (above). Turning Microwave Fried Chicken in a browning dish (left).

Converting Your Recipes

Conventional one-dish poultry recipes that call for cut-up pieces are easy to adapt for the microwave. Refer to the comparative chicken recipes to guide you in converting your favourite dishes. Here are some good tips to follow;-

☐ Butter- or oil-injected turkeys often have uneven concentrations of fat and thus cook unevenly. For best results, use uninjected turkeys.

☐ Poultry pieces prepared in a cream sauce should be cooked on ROAST to prevent the cream from separating or curdling.

☐ Chicken coated with a crumb mixture cooks to crispness more easily if left uncovered.

☐ Less tender game birds should be cooked on ROAST on a microwave roasting rack. Pour off fat as necessary. For best results, marinate game birds before cooking.

☐ Standing time is essential to complete cooking. Allow up to 15 minutes standing time for whole poultry depending upon size. The internal temperature will rise approximately 8°C/15°F during 15 minutes standing time. Chicken pieces and casseroles need only 5 minutes standing time.

Using the Defrosting Guide

1. Poultry can be defrosted within the original paper or plastic wrapping. Remove all metal rings, wire twist ties, and any aluminum foil. Since it is difficult to remove metal clamps from legs of frozen turkey, the clamps need not be removed until after defrosting. Be careful, of course, that the metal is at least 1 inch from the oven walls.
2. Place poultry in microproof dish while defrosting.
3. Defrost only as long as necessary.

Poultry should be cool in the centre when removed from the oven.

4. To speed defrosting during standing time, poultry may be placed in a cold-water bath.
5. Separate cut-up chicken pieces as soon as partially thawed.
6. Wing and leg tips and area near breast bone may begin cooking before centre is thoroughly defrosted. As soon as these areas appear thawed, cover them with small strips of aluminum foil; this foil should be at least 1 inch from oven walls.

DEFROSTING GUIDE—POULTRY

Food	Amount	Minutes (per pound)	Cook Control Setting	Standing Time (in minutes)	Special Notes
Capon	6-8 lbs.	2	Roast	60	Turn over once. Immerse in cold water for standing time.
Chicken, cut up	2-3 lbs.	5-6	Defrost	10-15	Turn every 5 minutes. Separate pieces when partially thawed.
Chicken, whole	2-3 lbs.	6-8	Defrost	25-30	Turn over once. Immerse in cold water for standing time.
Duckling	4-5 lbs.	4	Roast	30-40	Turn over once. Immerse in cold water for standing time.
Turkey	Under 8 lbs. Over 8 lbs.	3-5 3-5	Defrost Roast	60 60	Turn over once. Immerse in cold water for standing time.
Turkey breast	Under 4 lbs. Over 4 lbs.	3-5 1 2	Defrost Roast Simmer	20 20	Turn over once. Start at (roast), turn over, continue on (simmer).
Turkey drumsticks	1-1½ lbs.	5-6	Defrost	15-20	Turn every 5 minutes. Separate pieces when partially thawed.
Turkey roast, boneless	2-4 lbs.	3-4	Defrost	10	Remove from foil pan. Cover with paper.

Using the Cooking Guide

1. Defrost frozen poultry completely before cooking.
2. Remove the giblets, rinse poultry in cool water, and pat dry.
3. Brush poultry with browning sauce before cooking.
4. When cooking whole birds, place on a microproof roasting rack or an inverted microproof saucer in a glass baking dish large enough to catch drippings.
5. Turn over, as directed in Guide, halfway through cooking time.
6. Cook whole poultry covered loosely with a glass lid to prevent splattering. Toward end of cooking time, small pieces of aluminum foil may be used for shielding to cover legs, wing tips, or breast bone area to prevent over-cooking. Foil should be at least 1 inch from oven walls.
7. Cover poultry pieces with either glass lid or plastic wrap during cooking and standing time.
8. Standing time completes the cooking of poultry. Cooked whole birds may be covered with aluminum foil during standing time.

Poultry cooked in the Microwave Oven retains all its natural juices and flavours and the oven is much easier to clean after use.

☐ Poultry should be completely thawed before cooking.
☐ Place on a roasting rack, or upturned saucer and cover with a roaster bag.
☐ In order to prevent uneven cooking, protect legs and wings of poultry within strips of aluminium foil during cooking.
☐ When cooked, remove from oven and wrap in foil (shiny side inwards) for 15-30 minutes before serving.

COOKING GUIDE—POULTRY

Food	First Cook Control Setting and Time (in minutes)	Second Cook Control Setting and Time (in minutes)	Standing Time (in minutes)	Special Notes
Chicken, whole, 2-3 pounds	HIGH 3-4 per pound	Turn over. HIGH 4 per pound	5 (covered with foil)	Shallow baking dish, roasting rack, breast up.
3-5 pounds	HIGH 4 per pound	Turn over. HIGH 4-5 per pound	5	12×7-inch baking dish, roasting rack, breast up.
Chicken, cut up 2½-3½ pounds	HIGH 10	Turn over. HIGH 8-12	5	12×7-inch baking dish. Cover.
Chicken, quartered	HIGH 3-4 per pound	Turn over. HIGH 3-4 per pound	5	Shallow baking dish, skin side down.
Duckling 4-5 pounds	(Roast) 4 per pound	Turn over. Drain excess fat. (roast) 4 per pound	8-10	Shallow baking dish, roasting rack. Cover.
Turkey, whole, 8-14 pounds	HIGH 5 per pound	Turn over. (roast) 4 per pound	10-15 (covered with foil)	Shallow baking dish, 13×9-inch, roasting rack, breast up.
Turkey breast, 3-4 pounds	HIGH 7 per pound	Turn voer. (roast) 5 per pound		Shallow baking dish, roasting rack.
Turkey roast, boneless 2-4 pounds	(Roast) per pound	Turn over. (roast) 9 per pound	10-15	Loaf pan. Cover with plastic wrap.
Turkey parts, 2-3 pounds	(Roast) 7-8 per pound	Turn over. (roast) 7-8 per pound	5	Shallow baking dish with roasting rack.

COOKING GUIDE—CONVENIENCE POLUTRY

Food	Amount	Cook Control Setting	Time (in Minutes)	Special Notes
Precooked breaded chicken, frozen	1 piece 2 pieces 4 pieces 2-3 lbs.	Reheat	1-1½ 2-2½ 2½-3 10-12	Remove wrapping and place in microproof baking dish.
Chicken Kief, frozen	1 piece	Defrost HIGH	4-5 2½-3	Remove plastic wrap, place on microproof plate. First, thaw on 30 (defrost) and then, cook on HIGH.
	2 pieces	Defrost HIGH	6-7 4-5	
Chicken à la King, frozen	5 oz.	HIGH	3-4	Place on microproof plate. Stir before serving.
Creamed Chicken, Chicken and Dumplings, canned	7½-10½ oz.	Reheat	2-4	Stir once.
Escalloped chicken, chow mein, canned	14-24 oz.	Reheat	4-6	Stir halfway through cooking time.
Turkey tetrazzini, frozen	12 oz.	HIGH	3-4	Place on microproof plate. Stir before serving.
Turkey, sliced in gravy, frozen	5 oz.	HIGH	3-5	Place in microproof dish. Make slit in pouch before heating.

COQ AU VIN
COOKING TIME 21 MINS
1 Chicken (1½ kg/3 lb)—cut into 6 pieces
or:
6 Chicken Pieces
50 g/2 oz Butter
12 Onion Shallots
125 g/4 oz Chopped Bacon
125 g/4 oz cleaned, button Mushrooms
300 ml/½ pint Chicken Stock
1 Garlic Clove, crushed
2×15 ml spoon/2 tablespoons Cornflour
1 Bouquet Garni
125 ml/¼ pint Red Wine
Parsley

METHOD
☐ Melt the butter in a suitable container for 1 minute on HIGH.
☐ Add the chicken. Toss over in the butter. Arrange in dish in a single layer, cook uncovered on HIGH for 2 minutes, then turn and cook for a further 2 minutes.
☐ Remove the chicken, add the bacon, onions and mushrooms and cook for 2 minutes on HIGH.
☐ Mix cornflour with a little of the stock, then add with remaining stock, chicken, bouquet garni and red wine to casserole.
☐ Cover and cook for 15 minutes on HIGH or until chicken is tender.

CHICKEN CURRY
COOKING TIME 30 MINS
6 Pieces of Chicken
2×15 ml spoon/2 tablespoons Oil
1 Onion, finely chopped
2×15 ml spoon/2 tablespoons Curry Powder
1×5 ml spoon/1 teaspoon Chili Powder
1×5 ml spoon/1 teaspoon Salt
2×15 ml/2 tablespoons Tomato Puree
1×400 g/14 oz Can of Tomatoes

METHOD
☐ Place the chicken in a large but fairly shallow dish. Cook, covered for 10 minutes on HIGH.

☐ Combine the Oil, onions, spices and seasonings in a bowl and cook on HIGH for 5 minutes.
☐ Add the Tomato Puree tomatoes and juice, stir well.
☐ Add to the Chicken Pieces, cover and cook on HIGH for 15 minutes, stirring and turning the chicken pieces over once during cooking.
Leave to stand for 5 minutes before serving. Serve with rice and side dishes.

SWEET AND SOUR CHICKEN
COOKING TIME 12 MINS
500 g/1 lb Cooked Chicken, chopped
1×15 ml spoon/1 tablespoon Soy Sauce
2×level 15 ml spoon/2 level tablespoons of Cornflour
3×15 ml spoon/3 tablespoons Soft Brown Sugar
1×5 ml spoon/1 teaspoon Paprika
Pinch of Ginger
3×15 ml spoon/3 tablespoons Vinegar
1×15 ml spoon/1 tablespoon Tomato Ketchup
1×269 g/1×9½ oz Can Pineapple pieces
1 Green Pepper, de-seeded, sliced thinly
1 Carrot, cut into thin strips
1 Small Onion, chopped
4×15 ml spoon/4 tablespoons Water

METHOD
☐ Mix the soy sauce, cornflour, sugar, paprika, ginger vinegar, tomato ketchup, juice from the pineapple and water together in a suitable container. Cover and cook on HIGH for 1 minute. Stir well.
☐ Add the pepper, carrot and onion. Re-cover and cook for a further 6 minutes stirring frequently.
☐ Add the chicken and pineapple pieces. Cover and cook for 5 minutes on HIGH. Stir well before serving with rice or noodles.

ROAST CHICKEN
COOKING TIME 21½ MINS
1×1½ kg/3 lb Chicken
25 g/1 oz Butter
1×heaped 15 ml spoon/1 tablespoon paprika

METHOD
☐ Wash and dry the chicken.
☐ Melt the butter on HIGH for 30 seconds.
☐ Mix in the Paprika
☐ Brush this mixture over the chicken.
☐ Cover the chicken or place in a roaster bag and cook on HIGH for 21 minutes.
☐ Remove from the oven and keep covered. Leave to stand for 10-15 minutes.

DUCK A L'ORANGE
COOKING TIME 31 MINS
2 kg/4 lb Duckling
25 g/1 oz Butter
1 Orange

FOR THE SAUCE
Grated rind of 1 Orange
Juice of 2 Oranges
15 g/½ oz Cornflour
1×15 ml spoon/1 tablespoon Clear Honey

GARNISH
Orange Slices

METHOD
☐ Wash and trim the duckling. Pat dry with some absorbent paper.
☐ Rub over with butter.
☐ Stuff the neck cavity with orange segments.
☐ Cover or place into a roaster bag. Cook on HIGH for 28 minutes.
Leave to stand for 15 minutes.
☐ Place all the ingredients for the sauce in a jug and make up to 300 ml/½ pint with duckling juices and water. Mix well. Cook on HIGH for 3 minutes, stirring every minute. Pour over the duck and garnish with orange slices.

CHICKEN CACCIATORE
COOKING TIME 35 MINS
4 Medium sized Chicken Pieces
4×15 ml spoon/4 tablespoons Seasoned Flour
50 g/2 oz Butter
1×15 ml spoon/1 tablespoon Oil
1 Large Onion, peeled and finely chopped
1 Garlic Clove, chopped
397 g/1×14 oz Can of Peeled Tomatoes, chopped
1×5 ml spoon/1 teaspoon Sugar
150 ml/¼ pint Chicken Stock
125 g/4 oz Button Mushroom, washed and sliced
Black Pepper

METHOD
☐ Heat a browning dish for 6 minutes on HIGH or heat butter and oil in a suitable dish for 1 minute on HIGH.
☐ Toss the chicken in seasoned flour.
☐ Add the butter and oil.
☐ Add the chicken and brown for 2½ minutes on each side on HIGH.
☐ Remove and then add the onion and garlic. Cook until golden brown, 4 minutes on HIGH.
☐ Add any remaining flour, with the tomatoes, sugar, stock and mushrooms. Add black pepper to taste.
☐ Replace chicken, cover and cook on ROAST for 25 minutes.
☐ Serve with noodles, macaroni or spaghetti.
NOTE:
If you do not have a browning skillet, fry the chicken and onion in a suitable dish.

PAPRIKA CHICKEN
COOKING TIME 32½ MINS
1×1.5kg/3lb Chicken cut into 6-8 pieces
Seasoned flour
25g/1oz Butter
1 Medium Onion, sliced
450ml/¾ pint chicken stock
4×5ml spoon/4 teaspoons tomato puree
3×5ml spoon/3 teaspoons paprika
Salt and Pepper
250g/8oz Button Mushrooms, washed and
  sliced
150ml/¼ pint single or soured cream
Cornflour for thickening—optional
Parsley sprigs for garnishing

METHOD
☐ Toss the chicken in the seasoned
  flour and fry in a frying pan or
  preheated browning skillet until
  brown.
☐ Melt the butter in a large casserole
  dish on HIGH for 30 seconds.
☐ Add the onion and cook for 2 minutes.
☐ Add the chicken-stock, tomato puree,
  paprika, and seasoning and mix
  thoroughly.
☐ Add the chicken pieces and mushrooms and cook, covered on ROAST
  for 30 minutes stirring once during
  cooking.
☐ Remove chicken and stir in cream.
  Serve on a bed of rice.

CHICKEN AU VERONIQUE
COOKING TIME 17¾ MINS
500g/1lb Chicken
50g/2oz Butter
50g/2oz Plain Flour
300ml/½ pint Cider or White Wine
300ml/½ pint Chicken Stock
150ml/¼ pint Single Cream
125g/4oz Green grapes, deseeded and
  cut in half
Salt & White pepper

METHOD
☐ Cook the chicken on HIGH for 7
  minutes. Then cut into pieces and
  remove bones.
☐ Melt the butter on HIGH, for 45
  seconds.
☐ Mix in the flour, cider, chicken stock
  and seasonings.
☐ Microwave on HIGH for 5 minutes,
  stirring every minute to keep the
  sauce smooth.
☐ Add the chicken and grapes.
☐ Stir in the cream and pour into a
  serving dish.
☐ Cook on ROAST for 5 minutes until
  heated through.
☐ Leave to stand for 5 minutes and
  serve on a bed of rice.

CATCH OF THE DAY

Poaching and steaming have always been the most classic methods of cooking fish. Now, discover the newest "classic"—fish and shellfish microwave-style! So moist, tender, and delicious that you'll never want to cook seafood any other way. And all this with no elaborate procedures: no need to tie the fish in cheesecloth or use a special fish poacher. Shellfish steam to a succulent tenderness with very little water. If you think your microwave oven cooks chicken and meat fast, you'll be amazed at its speed with fish! For best results, fish should be prepared at the last minute. Even standing time is short. So, when planning a fish dinner have everything ready. *Then* start to cook.

Poached Salmon with Sour Cream Sauce is best prepared in an oval baking dish (top left). Oysters Rockefeller is a fine entrée or appetizer (top right). Lobster tails are arranged in a circle with the thinnest part at the center of the dish (above left).

Converting Your Recipes

If your family likes seafood only when it is fried crackly-crisp, surprise them with a new taste delight when you try traditional fish recipes cooked in the microwave oven. They'll swear fish has been pampered and poached by the most famous French chef. Use the cooking charts and the recipes as guides for adapting your own dishes. If you don't find a recipe that matches or comes close to the conventional recipe you want to adapt, follow this general rule of thumb: Begin cooking at roast or at HIGH for one fifth of the time the conventional recipe recommends. As in conventional cooking, the secret of seafood is to watch it carefully, since fish can overcook in seconds. It's best to remove it when barely done and allow standing time to finish the cooking. If you read these simple tips, you'll have excellent results:

☐ Most recipes that specify a particular variety of fish will work when any white fish is substituted. When a recipe calls for fresh or thawed frozen fish fillets, use sole, coley plaice, cod, scrod, or any similar fish.

☐ Cook fish covered unless it is coated with crumbs, which seal in the juices.

☐ When cooking whole fish, the dish should be rotated one-quarter turn twice during the cooking process to help provide even cooking. The odd shape of the fish requires this procedure.

☐ Fish is done when the flesh becomes opaque and barely flakes with a fork.

☐ Shellfish is done when flesh is opaque and just firm.

☐ Shellfish come in their own cooking containers which respond well to microwaves. Clam and mussel shells open before your eyes. Shrimp, crab, and lobster shells turn pink.

☐ All seafood recipes freeze well except where otherwise noted.

☐ You can use the browning dish for fillets or fish cakes. Preheat, add butter or oil and brown on one side for best results.

☐ To remove seafood odours from the oven, combine 1 cup water with lemon juice and cloves in a small bowl. Boil in the microwave oven for several minutes.

Using the Defrosting Guide

1. Frozen fish may be thawed in original wrapper. First discard any aluminum foil, metal rings, or wire twist ties.
2. Place fish on microproof dish. Remove wrapping when fish begins to thaw.
3. One pound of fish takes 5 to 6 minutes to nearly thaw on defrost.
4. To prevent the outer edges from drying out or beginning to cook, it is best to remove fish from oven before it has completely thawed.
5. Finish defrosting under cold running water, separating fillets.

DEFROSTING GUIDE—SEAFOOD

Food	Amount	Cook Control Setting	Time (in minutes)	Standing Time (in minutes)	Special Notes
Fish Fillets	1 lb. 2 lbs.	Defrost Defrost	4-6 5-7	5 5	Defrost in package on dish. Carefully separate fillets under cold water. Turn once.
Fish steaks	1 lb.	Defrost	4-6	5	Defrost in package on dish. Carefully separate steaks under cold running water.
Whole fish	8-10 oz. 1½-2 lbs.	Defrost Defrost	4-6 5-7	5 5	Shallow dish; shape of fish determines size. Should be icy when removed. Finish at room temperature. Cover head with aluminum foil. Turn once.
Lobster tails	8 oz. package	Defrost	5-7	5	Remove from package to baking dish.
Crab legs	8-10 oz.	Defrost	5-7	5	Glass baking dish. Break legs apart and turn once.
Crabmeat	6 oz.	Defrost	4-5	5	Defrost in package on dish. Break apart. Turn once.
Shrimp	1 lb.	Defrost	3-4	5	Remove from package to dish. Spread loosely in baking dish and rearrange during thawing as necessary.
Scallops	1 lb.	Defrost	8-10	5	Defrost in package if in block; spread out on baking dish if in pieces. Turn over and rearrange during thawing as necessary.
Oysters	12 oz.	Defrost	3-4	5	Remove from package to dish. Turn over and rearrange during thawing as necessary.

Using the Cooking Guide

1. Defrost seafood fully; then cook.
2. Remove original wrapping. Rinse under cold running water.
3. Place seafood in microproof baking dish with thick edges of fillets and steaks and thick ends of shellfish toward the outer edge of the dish.
4. Cover dish with plastic wrap or waxed paper.
5. Test often during the cooking period to avoid overcooking.
6. Method and time are the same for seafood with or without the shell.

COOKING/DEFROSTING GUIDE—CONVENIENCE SEAFOOD

Food	Amount	Cook Control Setting	Time (in minutes)	Special Notes
Shrimp croquettes	12 oz. package	Reheat	6-8	Pierce sauce pouch, place on serving plate with croquettes. Cover, turn halfway through cooking time.
Fish fingers frozen	4 oz. 8 oz.	Reheat Reheat	2-3 3½-4½	Will not crisp. Cook on serving plate.
Tuna casserole, frozen	11 oz. package	HIGH	4-6	Remove from package to 1-quart casserole. Stir once during cooking and before serving.
Shrimp or crab newburg, frozen pouch	6½ oz.	HIGH	4-6	Place pouch on plate. Pierce pouch. Flex pouch to mix halfway through cooking time. Stir before serving.

COOKING GUIDE—SEAFOOD AND FISH

Food	Cook Control Setting	Time (in Minutes)	Standing time (in minutes)	Special Notes
Fish fillets, 1 lb. ½ inch thick, 2 lbs.	HIGH HIGH	4-5 7-8	4-5 4-5	12×7-inch dish, covered.
Fish steaks, 1 inch thick, 1 lb.	HIGH	5-6	5-6	12×7-inch dish, covered.
Whole fish 8-10 oz. 1½-2 lbs.	HIGH HIGH	3½-4 5-7	3-4 5	Appropriate shallow dish.
Crab legs 8-10 oz. 16-20 oz.	HIGH HIGH	3-4 5-6	5 5	Appropriate shallow dish, covered. Turn once.
Shrimp, scallops 8 oz. 1 lb.	Roast Roast	3-4 5-7		Appropriate shallow dish, covered. Rearrange halfway.
Snalis, clams, oysters, 12 oz.	Roast	3-4		Shallow dish, covered. Rearrange halfway.
Lobster tails 1: 8 oz. 2: 8 oz. each 4: 8 oz. each	HIGH HIGH HIGH	3-4 5-6 9-11	5 5 5	Shallow dish. Split shell to reduce curling.

DEFROSTING & COOKING GUIDE

Food	Defrosting Time	Cooking Time	Special Notes
500 g/1 lb Bass (Whole)	3-5 min	5-7 min	Cover Head & Tail with foil and Cling Film
500 g/1 lb Cod	4-6 min	4-5 min	Cover with Cling Film
500 g/1 lb Cod Steaks	4-5 min	6 min	Cook covered
500 g/1 lb Coley Fillets	4-5 min	4-5 min	
500 g/1 lb Haddock	4-5 min	4-5 min	Cover with Cling Film
500 g/1 lb Halibut	4-5 min	4-5 min	Cover with Cling Film
500 g/1 lb Hake	3-5 min	6-7 min	Cover with Cling Film
500 g/1 lb Herrings	2-3 min	5 min	Cover with Cling Film
1 Kipper	1 min	1-2 min	Cover with Cling Film
200 g/7 oz Boil in bag Kipper Fillets	3 min	3 min	Pierce Bag
500 g/1 lb Mackerel	2-3 min	5 min	Cover with Cling Film
500 g/1 lb Plaice Fillets	2-3 min	4 min	Cover with Cling Film
500 g/1 lb Salmon	3-5 min	4-5 min	Cover with Cling Film
500 g/1 lb Sole	2-3 min	4 min	
500 g/1 lb Trout (Whole)	2-3 min	6-7 min	Cover Head & Tail with Foil

PLAICE WITH GRAPES
COOKING TIME 7 MINS
8 Small fillets of Plaice
175g/6oz Green Grapes
Seasoning
300ml/½ pint White Sauce
1×5ml spoon/1 teaspoon Lemon Juice
25g/1oz Fresh White Breadcrumbs
25g/1oz Grated Cheese

METHOD
- ☐ Butter a suitable dish.
- ☐ Trim the plaice fillets and arrange side by side in the dish.
- ☐ Wash and dry the grapes. Halve them and remove the pips.
- ☐ Sprinkle the grapes over the fish and season well.
- ☐ Add the lemon juice to the white sauce and mix in well.
- ☐ Season the sauce and pour over the fish.
- ☐ Sprinkle the surface with breadcrumbs and cheese and cook on HIGH for 5-7 minutes.
- ☐ Place under a hot grill to brown the crumbs and cheese.

TROUT WITH ALMONDS
COOKING TIME 11 MINS
4 Medium Sized Trout
Seasoned Flour
50g/2oz Butter
50g/2oz Toasted Flaked Blanched Almonds
2×5ml spoon/2 teaspoons Lemon Juice

METHOD
- ☐ Cut and clean the trout but leave the head on. Coat each in a little seasoned flour.
- ☐ Melt the butter in a suitable dish on HIGH for 2 minutes.
- ☐ Place the trout side by side in dish, making sure that both sides are covered in butter. Add lemon juice and almonds to butter in bottom of dish.
- ☐ Cook covered on HIGH for 9 minutes, turning over once.
- ☐ Transfer the fish to a hot serving dish, coating with juice and almonds. Garnish with lemon wedges and parsley sprigs.

SOUSED HERRINGS
COOKING TIME 7-8 MINS
4 Herrings, Cleaned and boned
Salt & Pepper
300ml spoon/½ pint Vinegar and Water
2×5ml/2 teaspoons mixed pickling spice
2 Bayleaves

METHOD
- ☐ Season the fish with salt and pepper and roll up from head to tail.
- ☐ Place in a large shallow dish. Pour over the vinegar and water, spices and bayleaves.
- ☐ Cook, covered on HIGH for 7-8 minutes.

Trout with Almonds →

PRAWN CURRY
COOKING TIME 12 MINS
Vegetable Oil for frying
1 Large Onion, peeled and finely chopped
1×15ml spoon/1 tablespoon Curry Powder
1×2.5ml spoon/½ teaspoon Chilli Powder
1×396g/14oz Can Tomatoes, sieved
250g/8oz Peeled Prawns, cooked

METHOD
☐ Place about 1×15ml spoon/1 table spoon of oil in a dish with the onion. Cook on HIGH for 2 minutes.
☐ Add the curry and chilli powder and cook for a further 2 minutes.
☐ Add the tomatoes and cook for 3 minutes.
☐ Add the prawns and cook for 5 minutes stirring once.
☐ Serve on a bed of rice with a selection of accompaniments, such as:
Mango Chutney
Sliced Bananas, topped with a little lemon juice
Sliced Onion, sprinkled with paprika
Peeled and diced cucumber, mixed with natural yoghurt.

HALBUT WITH PRAWNS
COOKING TIME 15½ MINS
4 Halibut Steaks
150ml/¼ pint White Wine or Stock
25g/1oz Butter
1 Small Onion, peeled and chopped
1 Green Pepper, deseeded and sliced
125g/4oz Button Mushrooms, washed and sliced
125g/4oz Peeled Prawns, cooked
Salt and Pepper

METHOD
☐ Place the Halibut and wine or stock in a dish and cook, covered in the oven on HIGH, for 5 minutes. Leave to stand for 5 minutes and drain.
☐ Melt the butter on HIGH for 30 seconds. Add the onions, pepper and mushrooms and cook for 5 minutes on HIGH.

☐ Add the wine or stock to the vegetables and place the Halibut on top. Season and cook, covered on HIGH for a further 3 minutes.
☐ Then add the prawns and cook covered for a further 2 minutes. Garnish with parsley.

LEMON STUFFED MACKEREL
COOKING TIME 10½-11½ MINS
4×175g/4×6oz Mackerel, cleaned and boned

FOR THE STUFFING
15g/½oz Butter
1 Small Onion, peeled and finely chopped
75g/3oz Fresh White Breadcrumbs
Finely grated rind and juice of 1 lemon
1×15ml spoon/1 tablespoon Freshly chopped parsley
Salt and pepper

METHOD
☐ Melt the butter on HIGH for 30 seconds.
☐ Add the onion and cook on HIGH for 3 minutes.
☐ Mix in the remaining ingredients.
☐ Lay the fish flat on a board and season to taste. Spoon the prepared stuffing into the fish and reshape.
☐ Transfer to a large shallow dish and cook, covered on HIGH for 7-8 minutes.

Lemon Stuffed Mackerel ➞

KEDGEREE
COOKING TIME 20-21 MINS
350g/12oz Smoked Haddock
250g/8oz Long Grain Rice
2 Boiled Eggs Finely Chopped
50g/2oz Melted Butter
Seasoning

METHOD
☐ Wash and wipe the fish. Cook on HIGH for 4 minutes. Then flake with a fork.
☐ Place the rice in a tall container with an equal quantity of boiling, salted water. Cover and cook on HIGH for 13-14 minutes.
☐ Combine the rice, haddock, butter and boiled egg together and reheat on HIGH for about 3 minutes. Garnish with parsley.

FISH AND POTATO PIE
COOKING TIME 10 MINS
FILLING
375g/12oz Cod, Coley
300ml/½ pint Cheese Sauce
2×5ml spoon/2 teaspoons Chopped Parsley
1×5ml spoon/1 teaspoon Lemon Juice
Salt and Pepper

TOPPING
750g/1½lb Potatoes, cooked
25g/1oz Butter
3-4×15ml spoon/3-4 tablespoons Milk
Salt and Pepper
Parsley and Tomato Slices, for garnishing

METHOD
☐ Place the fish on a dish and cover with cling film. Cook on HIGH for 6 minutes (4 minutes if using Haddock).
☐ Flake the fish and remove the bones.
☐ Mix with the other ingredients and season well. Place in a pie dish.
☐ Mash the potatoes. Add the butter, milk and seasoning. Beat until soft and creamy.

☐ Place carefully on top of filling and mark with fork.
☐ Place under a hot grill until golden brown and crisp.
☐ Serve garnished with parsley and tomatoes.

BAKED STUFFED HADDOCK FILLET
COOKING TIME 6 MINS
2 Fillets of Fresh Haddock (350g)
1 Quantity of Stuffing of choice, eg Parsley and Thyme, Mushroom and Lemon, about 50g/2oz when made up when made up
2 Large Tomatoes, Sliced
2×15ml spoon/2 level tablespoons Chopped Parsley
50g/2oz Melted Butter
Salt and Pepper

METHOD
☐ Place 1 fillet of fish, flesh side uppermost, in a buttered shallow microwave dish.
☐ Cover with stuffing.
☐ Place second fillet, skin side uppermost, onto the stuffing.
☐ Top with tomato slices and sprinkle with parsley.
☐ Coat with melted butter.
☐ Cook on HIGH for 6 minutes.
☐ Remove from oven and place under a hot grill until golden brown.

SOLE AU GRATIN
COOKING TIME 10-13 MINS
4 large Fillets of Sole
Butter

FOR THE SAUCE
25 g/1 oz Butter or Margarine
25 g/1 oz Flour
300 ml/½ pint Milk
75 g/3 oz Cheddar Cheese, grated

TOPPING
2×15 ml spoon/2 tablespoons Fresh
Breadcrumbs
25 g/1 oz Cheddar Cheese, grated

METHOD
☐ Place the fish in a large shallow dish
and dot with butter. Cook, covered
on HIGH for 4-7 minutes. Drain away
excess juices.
☐ Melt butter on HIGH in a large cooking
container for 30 seconds.
☐ Add the flour and gradually add the
milk. Cook on HIGH for 5 minutes,
stirring at the end of every minute.
☐ Add the cheese and return to the
Microwave for a further 30 seconds,
then beat until smooth.
☐ Pour the cheese sauce over the fish.
Sprinkle with the breadcrumbs and
cheese and brown under a hot grill.
☐ Garnish with parsley and tomato slices.

COQUILLES SAINT JAQUES
COOKING TIME 12 MINS
50 g/2 oz Butter
1 Small Onion, grated
50 g/2 oz Plain Flour
150 ml/¼ pint Milk
150 ml/¼ pint White Wine
8 Scallops about 50 g/2 oz each
  (Shelled Weight)
50 g/2 oz Cheddar Cheese, grated
1×5 ml spoon/1 teaspoon Salt
Pepper

METHOD
☐ Place the butter in a large bowl and
melt on HIGH for 30 seconds. Add
the onion and cook HIGH for 3
minutes.
☐ Stir in the flour and mix well, cook on
HIGH for 30 seconds.
☐ Gradually add the wine and milk.
Then add the mushrooms, scallops
and seasonings and stir well. Cook
on HIGH for 8 minutes, stirring
ocasionally until the scallops are
tender and the sauce has thickened.
☐ Transfer into individual scallop shells
and sprinkle with cheese.
☐ Brown under a hot grill.

A VISIT TO THE DAIRY CABINET

Eggs and cheese are great microwave partners; but they can stand by themselves, too. There's nothing quite like plain scrambled eggs or cheese fondue made in the microwave oven. From the simplest omeletts to fancy quiches, the microwave oven can enliven an ordinary breakfast, Sunday brunch, or any meal. The recipes in this chapter are perfect for unexpected guests any time of day. Just remember to have on hand a carton of fresh eggs and some Cheddar or Swiss cheeses that keep well. Then,

a little onion and seasoning are all you need to make a quick, easy, and delicious meal. One reminder: Do not hardboil eggs in the microwave oven. Pressure builds up inside the shell, which causes the egg to burst. Egg yolks should always be carefully pierced before cooking to prevent them from popping. Keep in mind that eggs and cheese are delicate ingedients; handle them with care and you will have delectable results.

Omelet Classique is cooked and served in the same dish (above left). Just a flip makes your Sunny Side Up Eggs become "Over Easy" if that's your preference (above). Refrigerated cheese can be quickly brought to room temperature at BAKE for 1 minute (left).

Converting Your Recipes

The best advice for adapting recipes that use eggs and cheese as primary ingredients is "better to undercook than overcook." Cheese and eggs cook so quickly that a few seconds can make the difference between airy excellence and a rubbery disaster. You will be able to make countless variations on the recipes here, substituting vegetables and cooked meat, and adding your own spices and sauces. Conventional soufflé recipes do not adapt to microwave cooking. Microwave soufflé recipes require a special form of stabilization because they cook so quickly; therefore, evaporated milk is used for the cream sauce base. The tips below will guide you to microwave success with all your egg and cheese recipes:

☐ Undercook eggs slightly and allow standing time to complete cooking. Eggs become tough when overcooked. Always check to avoid overcooking.
☐ Cover poaching or baked eggs to trap steam and ensure even cooking.
☐ Eggs are usually cooked at ROAST.
☐ If you want a soft yolk, remove the egg from oven before whites are completely cooked. A brief standing time allows whites to set without overcooking yolks.
☐ Cook bacon and egg combinations on HIGH, since most of the microwaves are attracted to the bacon because of its high fat content.
☐ OMELETTS and scrambled eggs should be stirred at least once during cooking. Fondues and sauces profit from occasional stirring during the cooking time.
☐ Cheese melts quickly and makes an attractive topping for casseroles and sandwiches.
☐ Cook cheese on ROAST or lower for short periods of time to avoid separation and toughening.

Using the Cooking Guides

1. Eggs should be at refrigerator temperature.
2. Eggs will continue to cook for 1 or 2 minutes after removal from oven, so remove just before done.
3. *To scramble:* Break eggs into a microproof bowl or 4-cup glass measure. Add milk or cream. Beat with a fork. Add butter. Cook at HIGH for time indicated in chart. Stir at least once during cooking from the outside to the centre. Let stand 1 minute before serving.
4. *To poach:* Bring water to a boil with a pinch of salt at HIGH. Break egg carefully into hot water. Pierce egg lightly with toothpick. Cook at ROAST for time required in chart. Let stand, covered, 1 minute before serving.

COOKING GUIDE—SCRAMBLED EGGS

Number of Eggs	Liquid (Milk or Creams)	Butter	Minutes to Cook
1	1 tablespoon	1 teaspoon	1 to 1½
2	2 tablespoons	2 teaspoons	2 to 2½
4	3 tablespoons	3 teaspoons	4½ to 5½
6	4 tablespoons	4 teaspoons	7 to 8

COOKING GUIDE—POACHED EGGS

Number of Eggs	Water	Container	Minutes to Boil Water	Minutes to Cook
1	¼ cup	6-ounce microproof custard cup	1½ to 2	1
2	¼ cup	6-ounce microproof custard cups	2	1½ to 2
3	¼ cup	6-ounce microproof custard cups	2 to 2½	2 to 2½
4	1 cup	1-quart microproof dish	2½ to 3	2½ to 3

COOKING GUIDE—CONVENIENCE EGGS AND CHEESE

Food	Amount	Cook Control Setting	Time (in minutes)	Special Notes
Omelette, frozen	10 oz.	Reheat	4-5	Use microproof plate.
Egg substitute	8 oz.	Simmer	4-4½	Turn carton over after 1 minute. Open carton after 1½ minutes. Stir every 30 seconds until smooth.
souffles: Corn, frozen	12 oz.	HIGH	10-12	Use 1½-quart casserole, covered. Rotate casserole twice.
Cheese, frozen	12 oz.	HIGH	11-13	Use 1½-quart casserole, covered. Rotate casserole twice.
Spinach, frozen	12 oz.	HIGH	12-15	Use 1½-quart casserole, covered. Rotate casserole twice.
Welsh rabbit, frozen	10 oz.	Roast	6-7	Use 1½-quart casserole, covered. Stir during cooking time.

FRIED EGG
COOKING TIME 1¼ MINS
1 Egg
Knob of Butter

METHOD
☐ Place butter on a saucer and heat on HIGH for 30 seconds. Break egg into dish.
☐ Prick yolk with a pointed knife.
☐ Cook covered for 45 seconds on ROAST. Leave to stand for 1 minute.

POACHED EGG
COOKING TIME 2½ MINS
1 Egg
1 small cup of Water

METHOD
☐ Bring the cup of water to the boil by cooking on HIGH for 1½ minutes. Carefully break egg into water.
☐ Cook covered on ROAST for 1 minute. Leave to stand covered for 1 minute.

SCRAMBLED EGGS
COOKING TIME 1½ MINS
2 Eggs
2×15ml spoon/2 tablespoons Milk
Seasoning

METHOD
☐ Mix together all ingredients.
☐ Cook on HIGH for 1½ minutes, whisk the mixture with a fork twice during the cooking.

SAVOURY OMELETTE
COOKING TIME 6½ MINS
25g/1oz Butter
1 Small Onion, chopped
1 Small Green Pepper, cut into slices
2×5ml spoon/2 teaspoons Olive Oil
3 Eggs
4×5ml spoon/4 teaspoons Cold Water
Salt and Pepper

METHOD
☐ Melt butter in a glass dish at least 2-5cm/1 inch in depth for 1 minute on HIGH.
☐ Add vegetables and oil. Cook covered on HIGH for 4 minutes.
☐ Beat the eggs, water and a pinch of salt together. Pour over the vegetables and cook uncovered for 1 minute on HIGH.
☐ Season to taste and stir bringing edges into centre. Cook covered for 30 seconds on ROAST.
☐ Stand for 1 minute before serving.

ITALIAN OMELETTE

For the vegetables use 1 small onion and 2 small courgettes and cook these in butter for 4 minutes on HIGH covered before adding egg mixture. Then cook as directed below.

HAM OMELETTE

Ingredients for plain omelette with the addition of 50g/2oz lean ham. Lightly fry in butter for 2 minutes on HIGH then add the egg mixture and cook as below.

METHOD

Melt butter in a shallow dish (a good idea is to use the lid of a casserole) for 30 seconds on HIGH. Beat eggs slightly and season them. Pour into dish and cover with a plate. Cook for 1 minute on HIGH. Uncover, stir eggs gently to bring edges into centre. Cook covered again on HIGH for 1 minute. Uncover and cook for 30 seconds on HIGH according to taste. Fold into three and serve hot.

CHEESE OMELETTE

Add 25g/1oz Grated Cheese, pinch of cayenne pepper and 1×15ml spoon/1 tablespoon cream to the beaten eggs and cook in the same way.

MUSHROOM OMELETTE

Make omelettes as directed before but sprinkle with 50g/2oz sliced mushrooms before cooking for the last 30 seconds.

SPANISH OMELETTE

25g/1oz Butter
1 Tomato, skinned and chopped
1 Small Potato, diced
Cook as for savoury omelette

QUICHE LORRAINE

COOKING TIME 8 MINS
2 Rashers Bacon, Chopped
1 Small Onion, Peeled and Finely Chopped
15g/½oz Butter or Margarine
50g/2oz Cheddar Cheese, Grated
150ml/¼ pint Milk or Single Cream
2 Large Eggs
20cm/1×8inch Baked Pastry Case

METHOD

☐ Place the bacon, onion and butter or margarine in a bowl and cook on HIGH for 2 minutes. Drain.
☐ Meanwhile, beat the eggs and the rest of the ingredients, together sprinkle bacon, onion and cheese into pastry case.
☐ Pour the mixture into the pastry case cook on HIGH for 6 minutes. Put under a hot grill to brown if liked.
☐ Garnish with tomato slices and parsley.

QUICK CURRIED EGGS

COOKING TIME 6 MINS
2×15ml spoon/2 tablespoons Oil
1 Onion, Chopped
1 Eating Apple, Chopped
1×15ml spoon/1 tablespoon Curry Power
1½×15ml spoon/1½ tablespoons Flour
300ml/½ pint Chicken Stock
1×15ml spoon/1 tablespoon Tomato Puree
4 Hard Boiled Eggs, Halved Longways
Salt and Pepper
Boiled Rice

METHOD

☐ Heat oil HIGH for 30 seconds.
☐ Add onion and apple and cook covered on HIGH for 4 minutes.
☐ Stir in curry powder and flour, cook for 1 minute on HIGH.
☐ Stir in stock.
☐ Bring to boil by heating on HIGH for 3 minutes stirring every 1 minute.
☐ Add puree and stir well.
☐ Place boiled rice on a serving dish, arrange eggs cut side up and pour sauce over, serve immediately.

MACARONI CHEESE
COOKING TIME 25 MINS

175g/6oz Macaroni
Generous Litre/2 pints of Boiling Water
1×5ml spoon/1 teaspoon salt
1×2.5ml/½ teaspoon Oil
50g/2oz Butter or Margarine
50g/2oz Plain Flour
600ml/1 pint Milk
175g/6oz Cheddar Cheese, grated
1×5ml spoon/1 teaspoon made mustard
Salt and Pepper

TO GARNISH
Paprika
Tomato, sliced
Parsley Sprigs

METHOD
☐ Place the Macaroni, water, oil and salt in a large mixing bowl. Cook on HIGH for 10 minutes, stirring twice during cooking. Drain and rinse.
☐ Melt the butter or margarine in a large mixing bowl and microwave on HIGH for 1 minute.
☐ Stir in the flour and gradually add the milk. Microwave on HIGH for 10 minutes, stirring every two minutes.
☐ Add the grated cheese, seasoning and mix in. Microwave on HIGH for 1 further minute.
☐ Add the macaroni and return to the microwave for a further 3 minutes on HIGH.
☐ Transfer to a serving dish. If desired brown under a hot grill. Sprinkle with paprika and garnish with tomato slices and parsley.

CHEESE FONDUE
COOKING TIME 6 MINS

500g/1lb Grated Cheese
1×15ml spoon/1 level tablespoon Cornflour
Black Pepper
Pinch of Nutmeg
300ml/½ pint White Wine
25g/1oz Butter
2×15ml spoon/2 tablespoons Kirsch
1 Loaf French Bread, cut into cubes

METHOD
☐ In a casserole dish combine cheese, cornflour, nutmeg and pepper.
☐ Heat the wine on HIGH for 3 minutes.
☐ Add to cheese mixture along with the butter. Cook covered on HIGH for 3 minutes, stirring every 30 seconds.
☐ After removing from oven stir well to finish melting the cheese and add the kirsch.
☐ Serve hot with cubes of french bread.

◄ Quiche Lorraine

THE GRAIN BELT

The microwave oven provides no significant saving of time when cooking pasta and rice. It takes just as long to rehydrate these products in the micorwave oven as it does conventionally. But the convenience of being able to cook and serve in the same dish, and to eliminate scorching and food stuck to pans makes it well worthwhile. Once the pasta is prepared and added to the rest of the ingredients according to the recipe, the casserole cooks in speedy microwave time. Another great advantage the microwave oven offers is that you can reheat pasta, rice, and cereal without adding water or having to stir. No worry about soggy noodles or starchy rice. And they taste as good reheated as when freshly cooked!

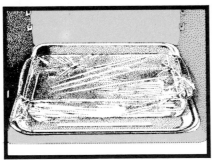

The microwave works wonders with pasta: simply top precooked macaroni or rotini with sauce, tomato slices, and cheese for a quick lunch (top left). Cook rice in boilable bags on a plate with the bag slit so steam can escape (top right). Spaghetti is cooked in a glass baking dish (above left). Hot cereal is now easy to prepare and serve right in the same dish (above right).

Converting Your Recipes

You will find that your conventional rice or noodle-based casseroles can be easily adjusted to microwave cooking. When you find a similar recipe here, adapt your ingredients to the microwave method, but follow only about three-quarters of the recommended micro-wave cooking times. Then check, observe, and extend the cooking time at 1-minute intervals until done. Make a note of the final cooking time for a repeat of the dish. By "trial" and trying to avoid "error," you'll soon be able to add to your collection of pasta and rice dishes. These tips will help;

☐ Casseroles cooked in the microwave oven usually need less liquid. Because of their shorter cooking time, there is less evaporation.

☐ Casseroles with cream and cheese sauces or less tender meats that require slow cooking do best on low settings.

☐ It is important to use a large microproof container when cooking pasta or rice to prevent water from boiling over.

☐ Thin noodles cook faster and more evenly than large noodles.

☐ Casseroles may require occasional stirring to distribute heat.

☐ Cook the ingredients of a casserole and stir before adding topping, such as cheese or bread crumbs.

☐ Cooked pasta or rice to be used in a casserole should be slightly firmer than if it is to be eaten at once. Simply cook for less time.

☐ Quick-cooking rice may be substituted in converting from conventional recipes that call for uncooked rice, in order to make sure the rice will cook in the same short time as the rest of the ingredients. Otherwise precook regular rice to a firm stage and add to the casserole.

☐ To reheat pasta, rice, and cereals in the microwave without drying out, cover tightly with plastic wrap. Set at reheat for just a few minutes, depending upon amount.

Using The Cooking Guides

1. For pasta, combine water with 1 tablespoon salad oil and 1 to 2 teaspoons salt in microproof container. Bring water to a boil on HIGH. Stir, Cover, Cook at simmer until done. Drain in colander, rinse in warm water. Serve.

2. For rice, add salt and margarine to water according to package directions. Bring water to full boil on HIGH. Stir in rice. Cover tightly. Cook on simmer for time provided in chart. Let stand, covered, 5 minutes before serving.

3. For quick-cooking cereal, follow chart and package recommendations. Stir after removing from oven. Let stand about 1 minute before serving.

COOKING GUIDE—PASTA

Food	Amount Uncooked (2oz.=1 cup)	Hot Tap Water	Time to Boil (in minutes) HIGH	Cook Control Setting	Time (in minutes)	Special Notes
Spaghetti or linguine	2 oz.	2½ cups	5-6	Simmer	5-6	Use 13×9×2-inch baking dish. Stir once.
	4 oz.	4 cups	8-10	Simmer	6-8	
	7 oz.	6 cups	12-14	Simmer	8-10	
Macaroni	5 oz.	3 cups	6-8	Simmer	10-12	Use 3-quart casserole.
Egg noodles, fine	2 oz.	2 cups	4-6	Simmer	5-6	Use 3-quart casserole.
Egg noodles, narrow	4 oz.	3 cups	6-8	Simmer	8-10	
Egg noodles, wide	8 oz.	6 cups	12-14	Simmer	12-14	
Lasagna noodles	4 oz.	4 cups	8-10	Simmer	12-14	Use 13×9×2-inch baking dish.
	8 oz.	6 cups	12-14	Simmer	14-15	
Spinach noodles	4 oz.	4 cups	8-10	Simmer	9-11	Use 13×9×2-inch baking dish.

COOKING GUIDE—RICE

Food	Amount Uncooked	Water	Minutes to Full Boil HIGH	Cook Control Setting	Time (in minutes)	Standing Time (in minutes)	Special Notes
Short-grain	1 cup	2 cups	4-5	Simmer	13-15	5	2-quart casserole
Long-grain	1 cup	2 cups	4-5	Simmer	15-17	5	2-quart casserole
Brown rice	1 cup	3 cups	6-7	Simmer	40	5	3-quart casserole
Quick-cooking	1 cup	1 cup	3-4	HIGH	0	5	1-quart casserole

COOKING/DEFROSTING GUIDE—CONVENIENCE RICE AND PASTA

Food	Amount	Cook Control Setting	Time (in minutes)	Special Notes
Rice, cooked refrigerated	1 cup	Reheat	1½-2	Use covered bowl. Let stand 2 minutes, stir.
Cooked, frozen	1 cup	Reheat	2-3	
	2 cups	Reheat	3-4	
Pouch, frozen	11 oz.	Reheat	6-7	Slit pouch.
Fried rice, frozen	10 oz.	HIGH	5-6	Use covered casserole. Stir twice. Let stand 5 minutes.
Spanish rice, canned	12 oz.	HIGH	4-5	Use covered casserole. Stir twice. Let stand 3 minutes.
Lasagna, frozen	21 oz.	Roast	19-20	Use covered casserole. Let stand, covered, 5 minutes.
Macaroni and beef, frozen	11 oz. package	HIGH	7-9	Use covered casserole. Stir twice.
Macaroni and cheese, frozen	10 oz.	HIGH	7-9	Use covered casserole. Stir twice.
Spaghetti and meatballs, frozen	14 oz.	HIGH	8-10	Use covered casserole. Stir twice.

COOKING GUIDE—CEREAL

Food	Servings	Amount Uncooked	Salt	Hot Tap Water	Setting	Minutes To Cook	Special Notes
Oatmeal, quick	1	⅓ cup	⅛ tsp.	¾ cup	HIGH	1-2	16-oz. bowl
	2	⅔ cup	¼ tsp.	1½ cups	HIGH	2-3	1½-qt. bowl
	4	1⅓ cups	½ tsp.	3 cups	HIGH	5-6	2-qt. bowl

RICE, PASTA AND NOODLES COOKING CHART

	COOKING FROM RAW ON HIGH POWER	DEFROSTING TIME	REHEATING TIME ON HIGH POWER
Long grain rice (250g/8oz)	Cook in 600ml/1 pint boiling salted water for 9 mins. Stand for 5 mins.	5 mins. Stand for 2 mins.	4 mins. Stand for 2 mins.
Quick cook long grain rice (250g/8oz)	Cook in 600ml/1 pint boiling salted water for 7 mins. Stand for 3 mins.	3 mins. Stand for 3 mins.	4 mins. Stand for 1 mins.
Brown rice (250g/8oz)	Cook in 600ml/1 pint boiling salted water for 20 mins. Stand for 3-4 mins.	7 mins. Stand for 3 mins.	4-5 mins. Stand for 1 min.
Savoury rice (125g/4oz)	Cook in 450ml/¾ pint boiling water for 18 mins. Stand for 3 mins.	4 mins. Stand for 2 mins.	2 mins. Stand for 1 mins.
Heat and serve rice (300g/9¼ oz)	Heat 150ml/¼ pint water and salt for 2¼ mins., add rice and cook for 3 mins. Stand for 2 mins.	—	—
Spaghetti (250g/8oz)	Add 1×10ml/1 dsp oil to 600ml/1 pint boiling salted water and cook for 13 mins. Stand for 2 mins.	6½ mins. Stand for 2 mins.	4 mins. Stand for 2 mins.
Lasagne (250g/8oz)	Cook in 600ml/1 pint boiling salted water for 14 mins. Stand for 2 mins.	6 mins. Stand for 3 mins.	4 mins., turn over once. Stand for 2 mins.
Macaroni (250g/8oz)	Add 1×10ml/1 dsp oil to 1.2 litres/2 pints boiling salted water	7 mins. Stand for 2 mins.	4 mins. Stand for 1 min.
Pasta shells (250g/8oz)	Cook in 1.8 litres/3 pint boiling salted water and cook for 18 mins.	7 mins. Stand for 2 mins.	4 mins. Stand for 1 min.
Egg noodles (250g/8oz)	Cook in 600ml/1 pint boiling salted water for 5 mins. Stand for 2 mins.	6 mins. Stand for 2 mins.	5 mins. Stand for 1 min.

Microwave cooking times are from the moment the water returns to the boil.

SPAGHETTI BOLOGNAISE
COOKING TIME 29 MINS
25g/1oz Butter
2×5ml spoon/2 teaspoons Olive Oil
50g/2oz Mushrooms, sliced
1 Small Onion, chopped
250g/8oz Minced Beef
2×15ml spoon/2 tablespoons Tomato
  Puree
227g/8oz Can Tomatoes, chopped
1×15ml spoon/1 tablespoon Red Wine
50g/2oz Spaghetti per person
Seasoning
Parmesan Cheese

METHOD
☐ Heat butter and oil on HIGH for
1 minute. Add mushrooms and
onion and cook covered for 2 minutes
on HIGH. Stir in meat, cook for
2 minutes.
☐ Add remaining ingredients and cook
HIGH for a further 5 minutes until
thickened stirring occasionally.
☐ Keep covered and leave to stand
while cooking spaghetti.
☐ Heat 2 pints salted water on HIGH
until boiling approx 10 minutes. Add
Spaghetti, cook on HIGH for 7
minutes.
☐ Serve immediately on warm plates,
pour over sauce and top with
parmesan cheese.

COMPLEMENTS FOR YOUR MEAL

You microwave oven enables you to enter one of the most exciting areas of the culinary arts: the world of succulent crisp-cooked vegetables. Because very little water is used, sometimes none at all, vegetables emerge from the microwave oven with bright, fresh colour, full of flavour, tender and nutritious. Even reheated, fresh vegetables retain their original flavour and colour. They do not dry out, because the steam that heats them is primarily generated within the vegetables themselves. Canned vegetables heat well too, because they can be drained before cooking so that they retain full fresh taste after cooking.

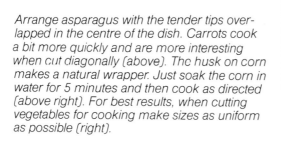

Arrange asparagus with the tender tips overlapped in the centre of the dish. Carrots cook a bit more quickly and are more interesting when cut diagonally (above). The husk on corn makes a natural wrapper. Just soak the corn in water for 5 minutes and then cook as directed (above right). For best results, when cutting vegetables for cooking make sizes as uniform as possible (right).

Converting Your Recipes

Vegetables are best when eaten at the crisp stage, tender but resilient to the bite. However, if you prefer a softer texture, increase water and cooking time. To adapt a conventional recipe to the microwave oven, find a similar recipe in the chapter and check the vegetable cooking guides. The following tips will give you additional help in adapting or creating your own recipes:

☐ Check cooking after the shortest recommended cooking times. Add more cooking time to suit individual preferences.

☐ If necessary, frozen vegetables may be used in recipes calling for fresh vegetables. It is not necessary to thaw frozen vegetables before cooking.

☐ Freeze small portions of your favourite vegetable dishes in plastic pouches. If you use metal twist ties, be sure to replace with string or rubber band before cooking. Cut a steam vent in pouch and reheat on microproof plate.

☐ To prevent boiling over when preparing vegetable dishes with cream sauces, use a baking dish large enough to allow for bubbling. Use a lower setting such as bake or roast.

☐ Celery, onions, green peppers, and carrots need to be partially cooked before adding to a casserole. In general, you should partially cook all vegetables before combining with already cooked meats, fish, or poultry.

☐ To cook mashed potatoes, cube potatoes, add a small amount of water. Cook tightly covered until soft. Season and mash.

☐ To reheat mashed potatoes, set at reheat, stirring once during cooking time.

☐ Because carrots and beets are fibrous, they may require more water and a longer cooking period to prevent dehydration and toughening during cooking.

Using the Cooking Guide

1. All fresh or frozen vegetables are cooked and reheated on HIGH.
2. Choose a wide, shallow dish so vegetables can be spread out.
3. Add ¼ cup water for each ½ to 1 pound fresh vegetables. Do not add water for washed spinach, corn on the cob, baked potatoes, or aubergine.
4. Do not salt vegetables until after cooking.
5. Cover all vegetables tightly.
6. Stir vegetables once during cooking time.
7. Pouches of frozen vegetables require steam vents. Slit pouch and cook on microproof dish.
8. Frozen vegetables without sauces can be cooked in their cartons without water. Remote waxed paper wrapping before placing carton in oven. (Remove frozen-in-sauce vegetables if packaged in cartons rather than pouches. Place in 1½-quart microproof casserole. Add liquid before cooking as package directs.)
9. After cooking, allow all vegetables to stand, covered, for 2 to 3 minutes.

COOKING GUIDE—VEGETABLES

Food	Amount	Fresh Vegetable Preparation	Time (in minutes)	Water	Standing Time (in minutes)	Special Notes
Artichokes 3½ in diameter	Fresh: 1 2 4 Frozen: 10 oz.	Wash thoroughly. Cut tops off each leaf. Slit pouch	7-8 11-12 5-6	¼ cup ½ cup	2-3 2-3	When done, a leaf peeled from whole comes off easily.
Asparagus: spears and cut pieces	Fresh: 1 lb. Frozen: 10 oz.	Wash thoroughly. Snap off tough base and discard.	2-3 7-8	¼ cup None	None 2-3	Stir or rearrange once during cooking time.
Beans: green, wax, French-cut	Fresh: 1 lb. Frozen: 6 oz.	Remove ends. Wash well. Leave whole or break in pieces.	12-14 7-8	¼ cup None	2-3 None	Stir once or rearrange as necessary.
Beets	4 medium	Scrub beets. Leave 1" of top on beet.	16-18	¼ cup	None	After cooking, peel. Cut or leave whole.
Broccoli	Fresh, whole 1-1½ lbs. Frozen, whole Fresh, chopped, 1-1½ lbs. Frozen, chopped 10 oz.	Remove outer leaves. Slit stalks.	9-10 8-10 12-14 8-9	¼ cup ¼ cup ¼ cup None	3 3 2 2	Stir or rearrange during cooking time.
Brussels sprouts	Fresh: 1 lb. Frozen: 10 oz.	Remove outside leaves if wilted. Cut off stems. Wash	8-9 6-7	¼ cup None	2-3 None	Stir or rearrange once during cooking time.
Cabbage	½ medium head, shredded 1 medium head, wedges	Remove outside wilted leaves.	5-6 13-15	¼ cup ¼ cup	2-3 2-3	Rearrange wedges after 7 minutes.
Carrots	4: sliced or diced 6: sliced or diced 8: tiny, whole Frozen: 10 oz.	Peel and cut off tops. Fresh young carrots cook best.	7-9 9-10 8-10 8-9	1 Tb. 2 Tbs. 2 Tbs. None	2-3 2-3 2-3 None	Stir once during cooking time.
Cauliflower	1 medium, in flowerets 1 medium, whole Frozen: 10 oz.	Cut tough stem. Wash, remove outside leaves. Remove core.	7-8 8-9 8-9	¼ cup ½ cup ¼ cup	2-3 3 3	Stir after 5 minutes. Turn over once. Stir after 5 minutes.
Celery	2½ cups, 1" slices	Clean stalks thoroughly.	8-9	¼ cup	2	
Corn: kernel	Frozen: 10 oz.		5-6	¼ cup	2	Stir halfway through cooking time.
On the cob	1 ear 2 ears 3 ears 4 ears Frozen, 2 ears 4 ears	Husk, wrap each in paper. Place on glass tray in oven. Cook no more than 4 at a time. Flat dish, covered.	3-4 6-7 9-10 11-12 5½-6 10-11	None None None None None None	2 2 2 2 2	Rearrange halfway through cooking time unless cooked on microproof rack. Rearrange halfway through cooking time.
Aubergine	1 medium, sliced 1 medium, whole	Wash and peel. Cut into slices or cubes. pierce skin.	5-6 6-7	2 Tb.	3	Place on micro-proof rack.
Greens: kale, etc.	Fresh: 1 lb. Frozen: 10 oz.	Wash. Remove wilted leaves or tough stem.	6-7 7-8	None None	2 2	

COOKING GUIDE—VEGETABLES

Food	Amount	Fresh Vegetable Preparation	Time (in Minutes)	Water	Standing Time (in minutes)	Special Notes
Mushrooms	Fresh: ½ lb., sliced	Add butter or water.	2-4	2 Tbs.	2	Stir halfway through cooking time.
Okra	Fresh: ½ lb.	Wash thoroughly. Leave whole or cut in thick slices.	3-5	¼ cup	2	
	Frozen: 10 oz.		7-8	None	2	
Onions	1 lb. tiny whole	Peel. Add 1 Tb. buter.	6-7	¼ cup	3	Stir once during cooking time.
	1 lb., medium to large	Peel and quarter. Add 1 Tb. butter.	7-9	¼ cup	3	
Parsnips	4 medium, quartered	Peel and cut.	8-9	¼ cup	2	Stir once during cooking time.
Peas: green	Fresh: 1 lb.	Shell peas. Rinse well.	7-8	¼ cup	2	Stir once during cooking time.
	Fresh: 2 lbs.		8-9	½ cup	2-3	
	Frozen: 6 oz.		5-6	None	None	
Peas and onions	Frozen: 10 oz.		6-8	2 Tbs.	2	
Pea pods	Frozen: 6 oz.		3-4	2 Tbs.	3	
Potatoes, sweet 5-6 oz. ea.	1	Scrub well. Pierce with fork. Place on rack or paper towel in circle, 1" apart.	4-4½	None	3	
	2		6-7	None	3	
	4		8-10	None	3	
	6		10-11	None	3	
Potatoes, white baked 6-8 oz. ea.	1	Wash and scrub well. Pierce with fork. Place on rack or paper towel in circle, 1" apart. in circle, 1" apart.	4-6	None	3	
	2		6-8	None	3	
	3		8-12	None	3	
	4		12-16	None	3	
	5		12-20	None	3	
russet, boiling	3	Peel potatoes, cut in quarters.	12-16	½ cup	None	Stir once during cooking time.
Spinach	Fresh: 1 lb.	Wash well. Remove tough stems. Drain.	6-7	None	2	Stir once during cooking time.
	Frozen: 10 oz.		7-8	None	2	
Turnips	4 cups cubed	Peel, wash.	9-11	¼ cup	3	Stir after 5 minutes.
Zucchini	3 cups sliced	Wash; do not peel.	7-8	¼ cou	2	Stir after 4 minutes.

COOKING GUIDE—CANNED VEGETABLES

Size	Cook Control Setting	Minutes Drained	Minutes Undrained	Special Notes
8 ounces	Reheat	1½-2	2-2½	Regardless of quantity: use a 4-cup
15 ounces	Reheat	2½-3	3-4	microproof casserole, covered. Stir once.
17 ounces	Reheat	3½-4	4-5	Let stand, covered, 2-3 minutes before serving.

COOKING GUIDE—CONVENIENCE VEGETABLES

Food	Amount	Cook Control Setting	Time (in minutes)	Special Notes
Au gratin vegetables, frozen	11½ oz.	Roast	10-12	Use glass loaf dish, covered.
Baked beans, frozen	6 oz.	Roast	8-10	Use 1½-quart casserole, covered. Stir once.
Corn, scalloped frozen	12 oz.	Roast	7-8	Use 1-quart casserole, covered.
Potatoes stuffed, frozen	2	Roast	10-12	Use shallow dish. Cover with waxed paper.
Creamed potato mix.	4-5 oz.	Roast	20-24	
Au gratin, frozen	11½ oz.	Roast	12	Use 1½-quart casserole, covered with waxed paper.
Instant mashed	3½ oz. packet	HIGH	5-6	Use covered casserole. Follow package directions. Reduce liquid by 1 tablespoon.
Peas, pea pods, chestnuts, frozen	10 oz.	HIGH	6-7	Place pouch on plate. Slit pouch. Flex once during cooking time to mix.
Stuffing mix.	6 oz.	HIGH	8	Use 1½-quart casserole, covered. Follow package directions.

Using the Blanching Guide

The microwave oven can be a valuable and appreciated aid in preparing fresh vegetables for the freezer. (The oven is *not* recommended for canning.) Some vegetables don't require any water at all and, of course, the less water used the better. You'll have that "fresh picked" colour and flavour for your produce. Here are some tips in preparing vegetables for blanching:

☐ Choose young, tender vegetables.
☐ Clean and prepare for cooking according to Cooking Guide.
☐ Measure amounts to be blanched; place by batches, in microproof casserole.
☐ Add water according to chart.
☐ Cover and cook on HIGH for time indicated on chart.
☐ Stir vegetables halfway through cooking.
☐ Let vegetables stand, covered, 1 minute after cooking.
☐ Place vegetables in ice water at once to stop cooking. When vegetables feel cool, spread on towel to absorb excess moisture.
☐ Package in freezer containers or pouches. Seal, label, date, and freeze quickly.

BLANCHING GUIDE—VEGETABLES

Food	Amount	Water	Approximate Time (in minutes)	Casserole Size
Asparagus (cut in 1-inch pieces)	4 cups	¼ cup	4½	1½ quart
Beans, green or wax (cut in 1-inch pieces)	1 pound	½ cup	5	1½ quart
Broccoli (cut in 1-inch pieces)	1 pound	⅓ cup	6	1½ quart
Carrots (sliced)	1 pound	⅓ cup	6	1½ quart
Cauliflower (cut in flowerets)	1 head	⅓ cup	6	2 quart
Corn (cut from cob)	4 cups	none	4	1½ quart
Corn-on-the-cob (husked)	6 ears	none	5½	1½ quart
Onion (quartered)	4 medium	½ cup	3-4½	1 quart
Parsnips (cubed)	1 pound	¼ cup	2½-4	1½ quart
Peas (shelled)	4 cups	¼ cup	4½	1½ quart
Snow peas	4 cups	¼ cup	3½	1½ quart
Spinach (washed)	1 pound	none	4	2 quart
Turnips (cubed)	1 pound	¼ cup	3-4½	1½ quart
Zucchini (sliced or cubed)	1 pound	¼ cup	4	1½ quart

RATATOUILLE
COOKING TIME 17 MINS
1 Medium Aubergine
250 g/8 oz Courgettes
1 Large Onion, peeled and sliced
3×15 ml spoon/3 tablespoons Olive Oil
1 Clove Garlic, crushed
1 Green Pepper, washed deseeded & Chopped
1 Red Pepper, washed, deseeded & Chopped
400 g/14 oz Can of tomatoes
Salt and pepper

METHOD
☐ Slice the aubergine and courgettes. Soak in cold salted water for 30 minutes. Drain.
☐ Combine the Olive oil, onion, garlic in a container and cook uncovered for 4 minutes on HIGH.
☐ Add the peppers, aubergine and courgettes and mix well. Cover and cook for 5 minutes on HIGH.
☐ Add all the remaining ingredients and continue cooking for a further 8 minutes on HIGH until the vegetables are tender.

TOMATO CASSEROLE
COOKING TIME 9½ MINS
25 g/1 oz Butter or Margarine
1 Onion, peeled & Finely sliced
75 g/3 oz Breadcrumbs
1×5 ml spoon/1 teaspoon basil
Salt & Pepper
250 g/8 oz Sliced Tomatoes
50 g/2 oz Cheese, grated

METHOD
☐ Melt the butter or margarine on HIGH for 30 seconds. Add the onions and cook on HIGH for 4 minutes.
☐ Mix in the breadcrumbs, basil and Seasoning.
☐ Place a layer of tomatoes in a greased dish, season and cover with some of the breadcrumb mixture and cheese. Continue this layering, finishing with breadcrumbs and cheese. Cook, covered on HIGH for 5 minutes. Garnish with parsley.

COURGETTE & TOMATO CASSEROLE
COOKING TIME 12 MINS
500g/1 lb Courgettes, sliced, sprinkle with
    salt 20 minutes before cooking
1×500g/1 lb Can of Peeled Tomatoes,
    roughly chopped
1×2.5ml spoon/½ teaspoon Dried Basil
½ Beef Stock Cube, crumbled
Salt & Pepper

METHOD
☐ Combine all ingredients together in a
    large dish.
☐ Cook, covered on HIGH for 12 minutes,
    stirring twice during cooking time.

POTATOES NORMANDE
COOKING TIME 13 MINS
500g/1 lb Potatoes
25g/1 oz Butter
150ml/¼ pint Milk
Seasoning to taste

METHOD
☐ Peel and wash the potatoes, cut in
    thin slices and arrange, overlapping
    in a well buttered high sided dish.
☐ Pour the milk and cover with the
    remaining butter, which should be
    cut into small pieces.
☐ Cook for 13 minutes on HIGH.

CAULIFLOWER CHEESE
COOKING TIME 19 MINS
1 Medium Cauliflower, trimmed
6×15ml spoon/6 tablespoons Water
300ml/½ pint Cheese Sauce
Seasoning
25g/1 oz Grated Cheese
Paprika

METHOD
☐ Cook the cauliflower with the water
    on HIGH for 13 minutes in a covered
    container.
☐ Drain, season and pour the hot
    cheese sauce over the cauliflower
    head. Sprinkle with grated cheese.
☐ Sprinkle with paprika and reheat on
    HIGH for 2 minutes.
☐ Or brown under a hot grill.

CHEESY STUFFED PEPPERS
COOKING TIME 11 MINS
4 medium sized Peppers
250g/8oz Cooked Rice
50g/2oz Chopped Ham
25g/1oz Cooked Mushrooms
125g/4oz Grated Cheddar Cheese
25g/1oz Butter
Salt and Pepper to taste

METHOD
☐ Cut tops off peppers and keep for
    lids. Remove inside seeds and
    membranes.
☐ Blanch the peppers for 1 minute on
    HIGH.
☐ Combine rice with cheese, ham and
    mushrooms.
☐ Season to taste.
☐ Stand peppers in a suitable dish.
☐ Fill with equal amounts of rice mixture.
☐ Put knob of butter on each.
☐ Cover and cook on HIGH for 10
    minutes.

Potatoes Normande ➡

BRAISED CELERY
COOKING TIME 14-20 MINS
1 Head of Celery
300ml/½ pint Boiling Chicken Stock
25g/1oz Butter
Freshly Ground Black Pepper
Salt
Chopped Parsley to garnish

METHOD
☐ Cut the celery into 5-7½cm/2-3 inch long strips.
☐ Place the chicken stock, butter, seasoning and celery into a large deepish dish.
☐ Cover, and cook on HIGH for 14-20 minutes, stirring half way through cooking. Sprinkle with parsley and serve hot.

VEGETABLE SUET PUDDING
COOKING TIME 14 MINS
SUET PASTRY
250g/8oz Self Raising Flour
125g/4oz Shredded Suet
Pinch of Salt

FILLING
250g/8oz Mixed Root Vegetables
  (carrots, swedes, turnips)
175g/6oz Streaky Bacon
1 Large Onion, peeled and finely chopped
1 Clove Garlic, crushed
Salt and Pepper
1×2.5ml spoon/½ teaspoon Mixed Herbs
75g/3oz mushrooms, sliced
2×15ml spoon/2 tablespoons Tomato
  Puree

METHOD
☐ Sieve flour. Stir in the suet and salt thoroughly.
☐ Add enough cold water to form a soft dough. Knead lightly.
☐ Roll out on a floured board and line a 2 pint (1.1 litre) greased pudding basin, leaving enough pastry for a cover.
☐ Peel the vegetables and cut into small pieces. Place in a suitable container with 1×15ml spoon/1 – tablespoon water. Cook on HIGH for 4 minutes.

☐ De-rind and chop up bacon. Cook with garlic and onion on HIGH for 3 minutes. Add the seasoning, herbs, mushrooms and puree. Mix well and cook for a further 2 minutes on ROAST.
☐ Mix the vegetables and water with the rest of the ingredients and fill the lined pudding basin.
☐ Top with the crust lid and cover with cling film. Cook on HIGH for 5 minutes.
☐ If preferred, a crisper crust can be achieved by placing in a hot oven 400°F/200°C, gas No 6 for about 15 minutes after cooking.

STUFFED JACKET POTATOES
COOKING TIME 17 MINS
4 Medium sized Potatoes
50g/2oz Butter or Margarine
4×15ml spoon/4 tablespoons Milk
Seasoning
50g/2oz Ham
50g/2oz Cheese, grated

METHOD
☐ Scrub potatoes well and dry on kitchen paper. Prick all over with a fork.
☐ Place the potatoes on absorbent paper and cook on HIGH for 10-14 minutes.
☐ Leave to stand for 5 minutes. Then split in half. Scoop the insides into a bowl and cream with butter or margarine and milk. Season.
☐ Chop the ham and add to the potato mixture with the cheese.
☐ Return the potato mixture to the potato shells. Reheat on HIGH for about 5 minutes.

Braised Celery →

VEGETABLE & CHEESE PIE
COOKING TIME 12½ MINS
25g/1oz Butter or Margarine
1 Onion, peeled and finely chopped
1 Green Pepper, deseeded and chopped
125g/4oz Cauliflower
198g/7oz Can Sweetcorn kernels, drained
1×400g/14oz Can of tomatoes, chopped
1×5ml spoon/1 teaspoon yeast extract e.g.
  marmite
175g/6oz Grated Cheese
50g/2oz Fresh White Breadcrumbs

METHOD
□ Melt the butter on HIGH for 30
  seconds.
□ Add the onion, pepper, and caulifower
  and cook, covered on HIGH for
  7 minutes.
□ Add the sweetcorn, tomatoes, juice
  and yeast extract. Stir well. Cook,
  covered for 5 minutes on HIGH.
□ Spoon half the mixture into an ovenproof serving dish and cover with
  half the cheese. Add the remaining
  vegetable mix and then top with a
  mixture of cheese and breadcrumbs.
  Brown under a hot grill.

NOTE:
Any left-over vegetables can be used in this
dish.

STUFFED PEPPERS
COOKING TIME 18 MINS
4 Small Green Peppers, or 2 Large, halved
  length ways
250g/8oz Minced Beef
1 Onion, Finely Chopped
50g/2oz Mushrooms, washed & Sliced
1×15ml/1 tablespoon Tomato Puree
Salt & Pepper

METHOD
□ Wash, and cut the top off the peppers.
  Remove seeds and white membrane.
□ Place the onion and beef in a con-
  tainer and cook uncovered for
  4 minutes on HIGH.
□ Add the mushrooms and cook for
  2 minutes on HIGH.
□ Add the Tomato Puree and seasoning.
□ Fill the peppers, and place in a
  shallow casserole dish. Cover and
  cook for 12 minutes on HIGH.
□ Stand for 5 minutes before serving.

STUFFED CABBAGE LEAVES
COOKING TIME 18½-20½ MINS
4 Cabbage Leaves washed and trimmed
25g/1oz Butter
1 Onion, peeled and finely chopped
250g/8oz Minced Beef
50g/2oz Mushrooms, washed and sliced
2×15ml spoon/2 tablespoons tomato
  puree
298g/10oz Can of Condensed Tomato
  Soup or 300ml/½ pint tomato sauce
Salt and Pepper

METHOD
□ Blanch the cabbage in boiling water
  on HIGH for 2-3 minutes and drain.
□ Melt the butter on HIGH for 30
  seconds.
□ Add the onion and cook on HIGH for
  3-4 minutes. Add the meat and
  mushrooms and cook on HIGH for 4
  minutes, stirring several times during
  cooking.
□ Add the tomato puree and seasoning,
  and cook on high for a further
  1 minute.
□ Divide the meat mixture between the
  cabbage leaves and roll up. Place in
  a large shallow dish. Secure with a
  wooden cocktail stick if necessary, and
  cover with the tomato soup or sauce.
  Cook covered on HIGH for 8 minutes.

POUR ON THE PRAISE

Sauces are simple in your microwave oven. No scorching, less stirring, and quick results. Sauces don't stick or burn as they do on the conventional range. They heat evenly and require less time and attention. You don't have to stir constantly or use a double boiler.

Just an occasional stir is all that is required to prevent lumping, and, if you like, a little beating after cooking will make a sauce velvet smooth. You can measure, mix, and cook all in the same cup, or in the serving pitcher itself. Try making a sauce the microwave way, and turn an ordinary food into an elegant treat.

Sauces are so easy! Steps in making Basic White Sauce (below) are illustrated.

Converting Your Recipes

All those sauces generally considered too difficult for the average cook are easy in the microwave oven. When looking for a sauce recipe similar to the conventional one you want to convert, find a recipe with a similar quantity of liquid and similar main thickening ingredient such as corn flour, flour, egg, cheese, or jelly. Read the directions carefully to determine procedure, timing, and cook control setting. Then, when you stir, notice the progress of the sauce, and remove when the right consistency is reached. Keep notes to help you the next time. The following tips will help:

☐ Use a microproof container about twice the volume of ingredients to safeguard against the sauce boiling over — so easy with milk- and cream-based sauces.

☐ Sauces and salad dressings with ingredients not sensitive to high heat should be cooked on HIGH. Basic White Sauce is an example.

☐ Bring flour and other starch-thickened mixtures to the boil and remove as soon as thickened. Remember, overcooking will destroy thickening agent and sauce will thin.

☐ You will notice that more flour or corn flour is required in microwave cooking than in conventional cooking to thicken sauces and gravies, since they will not be reduced by evaporation.

☐ Stirring quickly two or three times during cooking is sufficient to ensure even cooking. Too much stirring may slow cooking.

☐ When sauces require time to develop flavour or if they contain eggs, which might curdle, they should be cooked slowly, on simmer or even defrost. Don't allow delicate egg yolk sauces to boil.

☐ You can make your own special sauce by flavouring Basic White Sauce as desired. For example, add cheese, cooked mushrooms, cooked onions, your favourite spices, tomato paste, horseradish, etc.

BASIC WHITE SAUCE
COOKING TIME 5½ MINS
25 g/1 oz Butter or Margarine
25 g/1 oz Plain Flour
300 ml/½ pint Milk
Salt and Pepper

METHOD
☐ Melt the butter in a large bowl for 30 seconds on HIGH.
☐ Stir in the flour and gradually add the milk and mix together.
☐ Cook on HIGH for 5 minutes, stirring at the end of every minute, whisking if necessary.
☐ Season to taste.

VARIATIONS ON BASIC WHITE SAUCE
Add the following at the end of cooking time and cook for a further 30 seconds.
ANCHOVY SAUCE
(For Fish Dishes)
2×5 ml spoon/2 teaspoons Anchovy Essence
CAPER SAUCE
(For Mutton, Lamb and Fish)
1×15 ml spoon/1 tablespoon Capers and
1×5 ml/1 teaspoon Caper Vinegar.
CHEESE SAUCE
(For main dishes, vegetables and fish)
75 g/3 oz grated cheddar cheese and
1×2.5 ml spoon/½ teaspoon made mustard.

EGG SAUCE
(Serve with fish, veal and poultry)
1 finely chopped hard boiled egg
MUSTARD SAUCE
(For white fish)
2×5 ml spoon/2 teaspoons made mustard
ONION SAUCE
(For lamb, mutton, tripe and boiled bacon)
2 large boiled and chopped onions
PARSLEY SAUCE
(For vegetables, fish, lamb, ham and boiled bacon)
2×15 ml spoon/2 tablespoons finely chopped parsley

CUSTARD SAUCE
COOKING TIME 5 MINS
2 Eggs, size 2
25 g/1 oz Caster Sugar
300 ml/½ pint Milk
Grated Nutmeg

METHOD
☐ Beat the eggs and sugar together in a bowl.
☐ Heat the milk and nutmeg on HIGH for 2 minutes.
☐ Pour the milk onto eggs, stir and strain the custard into a serving jug. Cook for 3 minutes. Whisk well at the end of every minute.

BECHAMEL SAUCE
COOKING TIME 37½ MINS
300ml/½ pint Milk
1 Carrot, peeled and sliced
1 Onion, peeled and chopped
6 Pepper corns
Blade of Mace
25g/1oz Butter or Margarine
25g/1oz Flour
Seasoning

METHOD
☐ Heat the milk on HIGH for 2 minutes and steep the vegetables and spices in it for 30 minutes. Strain.
☐ Melt the butter on HIGH for 30 seconds.
☐ Add the flour and gradually add the milk. Cook on HIGH for 5 minutes stirring at the end of every minute.
☐ Season to taste with salt and pepper.

TOMATO SAUCE
COOKING TIME 3½ MINS
25g/1oz Margarine
25g/1oz Plain Flour
250g/8oz Can Of Tomatoes, sieved and made up with water to 300ml/½ pint
1×15ml spoon/1 tablespoon Tomato Puree
1 Bay Leaf
Salt and Pepper

METHOD
☐ Place the margarine in a bowl and cook on HIGH for 30 seconds.
☐ Stir in the flour and gradually add the tomatoes and other ingredients. Re-cook on HIGH for 3 minutes stirring well at the end of each minute.
☐ Remove bay leaf.
☐ Serve with meat, fish or pasta dishes.

CHOCOLATE SAUCE
COOKING TIME 1-2 MINS
50g/2oz Plain Chocolate, broken into squares
15g/½oz Butter
1×15ml spoon/1 tablespoon Milk

METHOD
☐ Place the chocolate and butter a jug and heat on HIGH for 1-2 minutes.
☐ Add the milk and stir until smooth. Serve with ice-cream, profiteroles, poached pears.

APPLE SAUCE
COOKING TIME 5 MINS
250g/8oz Cooking Apples
15g/½oz Butter
1×10ml spoon/1 desertspoon Sugar

METHOD
☐ Peel, core and slice the apples. Place in a container with 1×15ml/1 tablespoon Water. Cook, covered for 5 minutes on HIGH.
☐ Remove from the oven and stir until smooth, use a fork if necessary. Add the butter and sugar and mix well. Serve with pork.

PRESERVES
Jams, Marmalade, Lemon Curd and Chutneys are all easy to cook in a Microwave Oven and will not leave you with a messy saucepan and sticky cooker through the jam etc. boiling over.

TESTING FOR A SET
There are several methods which may determine when jam or marmalade has reached a setting point.
THE TEMPERATURE TEST—a temperature of 110°C/220°F should be reached.
FLAKE TEST—Dip a wooden spoon into the jam or marmalade and turn the spoon, allowing the jam or marmalade to drop from it. If the jam or marmalade has been cooked long enough it will partly set on the spoon and the drops will run together to form flakes which hang from the spoon.
SAUCER TEST—place a little jam or marmalade onto a cold saucer and leave to cool. Push your finger across the top of the jam and the surface should wrinkle.

STRAWBERRY PRESERVE
COOKING TIME 17 MINS
(YIELD 500 g-1 kg/1-2 LB)
500 g/1 lb Strawberries
2×15 ml spoon/2 Tablespoon Lemon Juice
500 g/1 lb Sugar

METHOD
☐ Hull the strawberries, then rinse and dry thoroughly.
☐ Mix the strawberries and lemon juice together in a large bowl. Cook, covered on HIGH for 5-6 minutes until the strawberries are soft.
☐ Add the sugar, stir until dissolved and cook uncovered for 12 minutes until a setting point is reached.
☐ Leave to cool slightly, then pour into warm sterilized jars. Seal.

BLACKCURRANT JAM
COOKING TIME 20 MINS
(YIELD 500 g-1 kg/1 lb-2 lb)
500 g/1 lb Frozen Blackcurrants
500 g/1 lb Sugar
1×15 ml/1 tablespoon Lemon Juice

METHOD
☐ Place the frozen blackcurrants in a large Microwave proof bowl and cook on HIGH for 5 minutes. Leave to stand for 5 minutes.
☐ Stir in the sugar and lemon juice and cook on HIGH for 15 minutes or until a setting point has been reached. Stir twice during cooking.
☐ Pot in sterilized jars and cover.

RHUBARB AND GINGER JAM
COOKING TIME 30-35 MINS
(YIELD 1 kg-2 kgs/2 lb-3 lb)
1 kg/2 lb Rhubarb, cleaned and cut up
750 g/1½ lb Sugar
1×15 ml spoon/1 tablespoon Lemon Juice
2×5 ml spoon/2 teaspoons ground ginger

METHOD
☐ Place the rhubarb and sugar in layers in a large bowl and leave to stand overnight.
☐ Add the lemon juice and ginger to the rhubarb & sugar and mix thoroughly. Cook on HIGH for 30-35 minutes until a setting point is reached.
☐ Pot into sterilized jars and cover.

THREE FRUIT MARMALADE
COOKING TIME 50 MINS
Yield 2½-2¾kg/5-6lb
2 medium Lemons
2 medium Grapefruits
2 medium Oranges
900ml/1½ pints Boiling Water
2kg/4lbs Preserving Sugar or granulated sugar

METHOD
- [ ] Wash and dry fruit.
- [ ] Cut in half, squeeze out the juice and reserve.
- [ ] Remove pips and pith, and tie in a piece of muslin.
- [ ] Chop peel according to taste; fine, medium, coarse.
- [ ] Place juice, bag of pith and pips, with the peel into a large mixing bowl. Add the boiling water and cover with cling film, making slits in it to release the steam.
- [ ] Cook in microwave for 20-30 minutes, depending on the coarseness of the peel.
- [ ] Uncover and stir in the sugar. Cook uncovered for 30-40 minutes OR until setting point is reached. Stir every five minutes.
- [ ] Pot into sterilized jars — cover and label.

GRAPEFRUIT MARMALADE
COOKING TIME 55 MINS
(YIELD 2½-2¾kg/5-6lb)
1kg/2lb Grapefruit
Pips and juice of 2 Lemons
1.2 litres/2 pints Boiling Water
2kg/4lb preserving or granulated sugar, warmed

METHOD
- [ ] Wash the grapefruit well.
- [ ] Remove the rind and cut into thin strips. Remove all pips and pith from the grapefruit.
- [ ] Tie all the pips and pith in a clean piece of muslin.
- [ ] Coarsely chop the grapefruit flesh and place in a large mixing bowl with the muslin bag, lemon juice and water.
- [ ] Cover and cook on HIGH for 25 minutes, or until the peel has softened.
- [ ] Remove the muslin bag and allow to cool slightly. Squeeze the bag over the cooked fruit to remove as much juice and pectin as possible, then discard.
- [ ] Add the warmed sugar, stir thoroughly to make sure that the sugar has dissolved properly.
- [ ] Return the bowl to the oven and cook on HIGH for 30-40 minutes or until a setting point is reached. Stir every 5 minutes.
- [ ] When set, allow to stand for 5 minutes, then pot and cover, in sterilized jars. Label.

LEMON CURD
COOKING TIME 6½ MINS
(YIELD ½kg/1lb)
2 Lemons, rind and juice
3 Eggs, beaten
50g/2oz Butter
250g/8oz Granulated Sugar

METHOD
- [ ] Wash and dry the lemons. Grate the rind from each thinly. Squeeze out all the juice.
- [ ] In a medium sized bowl, heat the butter for 1½ minutes on HIGH.
- [ ] Add the remaining ingredients and beat together.
- [ ] Cook uncovered on HIGH for 5 minutes stirring well at the end of every minute. When cooked, the curd should be thick enough to coat the back of a wooden spoon.
- [ ] Pot and cover in a sterilized warm jar. Label.

APPLE & ONION CHUTNEY
COOKING TIME 45 MINS
(YIELD 3 kg/6 lb)
1 kg/2 lb Apples, peeled and chopped
1 kg/2 lb Onions, peeled and chopped
250 g/8 oz Sultanas
Juice and rind of 2 lemons
450 ml/¾ pint malt vinegar
1 Garlic Clove, crushed
500 g/1 lb Brown sugar

METHOD
☐ Place all the ingredients except the brown sugar in a large cooking container. Cover and cook on HIGH for 15 minutes.
☐ Add the sugar, cover and bring to the boil, and then cook covered on HIGH for about 30 minutes, until thick.
☐ Pot and cover.

TOMATO CHUTNEY
COOKING TIME 30-35 MINS
(YIELD 1-1.5 kg/2-3 lb)
1 kg/2 lb Ripe Tomatoes
250 g/8 oz Onions, peeled and chopped
1×5 ml spoon/1 teaspoon Salt
1×5 ml spoon/1 teaspoon paprika
1×2.5 ml spoon/½ teaspoon Ground Ginger
125 g/4 oz Brown Sugar
300 ml/½ pint Vinegar

METHOD
☐ Peel the tomatoes, chop roughly and place in a large bowl.
☐ Add the remaining ingredients and cook on HIGH for 30-35 minutes or until the chutney is thick and well blended.
☐ Pour into sterilized jars, seal and cover.

APRICOT CHUTNEY
COOKING TIME 29 MINS
(YIELD 2 kg/4 lb)
250 g/8 oz Dried Apricots
500 g/1 lb Apples, peeled and chopped
125 g/4 oz Sultanas
Juice and Rind of one lemon
1×5 ml spoon/1 teaspoon Salt
3×5 ml spoon/3 teaspoons Pickling Spices
600 ml/1 pint Malt Vinegar
500 g/1 lb Soft Brown Sugar

METHOD
☐ Chop the apricots into small pieces and place in a bowl with boiling water. Microwave on HIGH for 3 minutes. Leave to stand for 5 minutes or soak overnight. Drain.
☐ Place in a large container with the remaining ingredients except the sugar and pickling spices. Place the pickling spices in a muslin bag, tie up and add to the container. Cook on HIGH for 9 minutes, or until the apples are soft.
☐ Add the sugar and stir well. Bring the chutney to the boil, 2 minutes on HIGH and cook on HIGH for 15 minutes.
☐ Remove pickling spices, pot and cover.

A BAKER'S DOZEN

Treat your family and friends to the rich aromas of hot-from-the-oven bread, sweet rolls, muffins, and coffee cakes. For a quick and easy surprise breakfast or coffee break, count on the short cooking time of the microwave oven. Bread cooked in the microwave has an excellent texture and flavour, but does not brown or develop crust—there is no hot air to dry the surface as in conven-tional baking. For best results, if you like the browned look for your bread and muffins, use dark flours, molasses, and spices. Because a crust doesn't form, bread cooked in the microwave oven has the remarkable characteristic of rising higher than in conventional cook-ing. With tender, loving care you'll soon succeed in making homemade bread, muffins, and sweet rolls a constant addition to your menus.

Breads, and cakes are tested as in conventional cooking (above left). Custard cups arranged in a circle may be used to make cakes (above). Proofing bread is simple. A cup of water helps provide a moist environment (left).

Converting Your Recipes

When adapting "quick bread" recipes you will find it necessary to reduce the amount of leavening (baking powder or soda) by about onequarter the normal amount. A bitter aftertaste is apparent if too much leavening is used in biscuits or cakes. Since foods rise higher in the microwave oven, you will not see a loss in volume from the reduction of soda or baking powder. If a recipe contains buttermilk or sour cream, do not change the amount of soda, since it serves to counteract the sour taste and does not act only as a leavening agent. When using a mix where leavening cannot be reduced, if you allow the batter or dough to stand about 10 minutes before cooking, some of the gas will be lost. Yeast doughs need not be changed but may cook more evenly if cooked in a ring mould shape rather than the conventional loaf pan. And observe the following tips:

☐ Because breads rise higher than in a conventional oven, use a larger loaf pan to accommodate the volume.

☐ Fill paper-lined cake only half full to allow for cakes rising more.

☐ You can prepare your own "brown 'n serve" breads and rolls by baking them ahead in the microwave oven. Then place them in the conventional oven to brown just before serving.

☐ Breads and rolls should be reheated to the point where they are warm to the touch. Overheating or overcooking makes bread tough and rubbery.

☐ Heat' bread slices on paper napkins or paper towels to absorb excess moisture. You can heat bread and rolls on a microproof roasting rack as well. Or you can heat them on a paper napkin-lined basket and serve them right from the oven.

☐ When making yeast bread in a microwave oven, choose a recipe with cornmeal, whole wheat flour, or rye flour to achieve a rich colour.

COOKING/WARMING/DEFROSTING GUIDE— CONVENIENCE BREADS

Food	Amount	Cook Control Setting	Time	Special Notes
Hamburger buns, hot dog rolls, frozen	1 lb.	Defrost	3½-4½ minutes	Use original microproof container, paper plate, or towels. Place on microproof rack, turn over after 2 minutes.
Room temperature:	1	Reheat	5-10 seconds	
	2	Reheat	10-15 seconds	
	4	Reheat	15-20 seconds	
	6	Reheat	20-25 seconds	
Doughnuts, sweet rolls, muffins	1	Reheat	10-15 seconds	Place on paper plate or towel. Add 15 seconds if frozen.
	2	Reheat	20-25 seconds	
	4	Reheat	35-40 seconds	
	6	Reheat	45-50 seconds	
Whole coffee cake, frozen	10-13 oz.	Reheat	1½-2 minutes	Place on paper plate or towel.
Room temperature:	10-13 oz.	Reheat	1-1½ minutes	Place on paper plate or towel.
French bread, frozen	1 lb.	Reheat	1½-2 minutes	Place on paper plate or towel.
Room temperature:	1 lb.	Reheat	20-30 seconds	
English muffins, waffles, frozen	2	HIGH	30-45 seconds	Place on paper towels. Toast in toaster after defrosting, if desired.

COOKING/WARMING/DEFROSTING GUIDE— CONVENIENCE BREADS

Food	Amount	Cook Control Setting	Time	Special Notes
Blueberry muffin mix.	4	HIGH	1¼-1½ minutes	Use paper-lined custard cups or microproof
	6	HIGH	2-3 minutes	muffin tray. Let stand 2 minutes before serving.
Bread, frozen	1 slice	Defrost	15-20 seconds	Place on paper plate or towels. Let stand 5 minutes before serving.
	1 lb. loaf	Defrost	2-3 minutes	In original plastic bag, remove twister. Let stand 5 minutes before serving.
Coffeecake mix.	19 oz.	Simmer	10 minutes	Use 9" round dish. Turn dish if rising unevenly.
		HIGH	5-6 minutes.	Let stand 5 minutes before serving.

WHITE BREAD
COOKING TIME 2½ MINS
500g/1lb Strong Plain Flour
12g/½oz Salt
1×5ml spoon/1 teaspoon Dried Yeast
1×5ml spoon/1 teaspoon Sugar
300ml/½ pint Water
25g/1oz Butter

METHOD
☐ In a small dish mix sugar with ⅓ of the water and warm in microwave for 30 seconds on ROAST. Stir in yeast. Leave to activate, about 10 minutes.
☐ Mix the flour and salt and warm in microwave for 30 seconds again on LOW.
ROAST.
☐ Rub in butter. Mix to a dough with the yeast liquid and remaining water.

Knead thoroughly for 10 minutes.
☐ Return to a clean well greased bowl and cover with oiled cling film. Put in microwave for 15 seconds on DEFROST.
☐ Leave in a warm place for 5 minutes. Repeat 4 times until dough has doubled in size.
☐ Knead on a lightly floured surface for 5 minutes. Shape to fit a well greased 2lb loaf tin. Place inside a large well oiled polythene bag and leave in a warm place until loaf has risen.
☐ Remove polythene bag and leave in a warm place until loaf has risen, (brush with beaten egg if a crisp crust is required) and bake in a preheated oven, 230°C/450°F for 15 to 20 minutes until golden brown.

ICED BUNS
250g/8oz White Bread Dough
Glace Icing

METHOD
☐ Make up sweet dough as directed.
☐ After proving, split into 15 portions and shape into balls.
☐ Leave to prove again covered in a warm place for 15 minutes.
☐ Bake in a hot oven 220°C/425°F, gas mark No. 7 for 10-15 minutes.
☐ When cool spread top with glace icing.

DEVONSHIRE SPLITS
250g/8oz White Bread Dough
Jam
Cream
Icing Sugar

METHOD
☐ Make as for iced buns with same amount of sweet dough, and split into 15 sections.
☐ When cool, split into two and fill with fresh cream and jam.
☐ Dredge top with icing sugar.

PACKET BREAD MIX
☐ Make up dough as directed on packet and knead well.
☐ Cover with cling film and prove in microwave oven for 20 seconds on ROAST leaving a 10 second interval between each 5 seconds of cooking.
☐ Leave in a warm place to double in size.
☐ Preheat oven to whatever temperature is required and cook bread as instructed.

CURRANT BREAD
250g/8oz Strong Plain Flour
Pinch of Salt
50g/2oz Margarine
25g/1oz Sugar
1 Egg
4×15ml spoon/4 tablespoons Warm Water
2×5ml spoon/2 teaspoons Dried Yeast and 1×5ml spoon sugar/1 teaspoon Sugar
125/4oz Currants

METHOD
☐ Make a dough as directed above adding fruit when adding yeast and egg mixture. Prove as directed.
☐ After proving, split dough into three and plait together. Place in a greased tin and leave to rise for 15 minutes in a warm place.
☐ Bake in a preheated oven 400°F/200°C, gas No. 6 for 35-40 minutes.

WHEATGERM BREAD
COOKING TIME 11 MINS
225ml/⅓ pint Water, warmed to approximately 30°C/85°F
1×5ml spoon/1 teaspoon active dried Yeast
50g/2oz Soft Dark Brown Sugar
2×15ml spoon/2 tablespoons Cooking Oil
1×2.5ml spoon/½ teaspoon Salt
1 Egg, size 2
37g/1½oz Natural Wheatgerm
300g/10oz Brown Flour—wheatgerm

METHOD
☐ Using a large mixing bowl, combine water and yeast. Stir in sugar, oil, salt, egg, wheatgerm and about 225g/7oz of the flour.
☐ Beat this mixture for about 3 minutes then stir in the remaining flour to form stiff batter.
☐ Cover mixture and let it rise in a warm place until light and doubled in size, (approximately 1¼ hours).
☐ Stir batter down and spread in a 1.1 litre/2 pint ungreased dish. Cover again and let it rise in a warm place.
☐ Cook uncovered for 6 minutes on DEFROST and then on HIGH for 5 minutes.
☐ Take out of dish after loosening edges and place on a cooling tray.

SWISS ROLL
COOKING TIME 3-4 MINS
2 Eggs
50g/2oz Caster Sugar
50g/2oz Self Raising Flour, Sieved
Jam
Caster Sugar

METHOD
☐ Line a swiss roll dish with greased paper.
☐ Whisk eggs and sugar until thick and creamy.
☐ Add flour lightly with metal spoon. Pour into greased and lined dish.
☐ Cook on HIGH for 3-4 minutes. Do not overcook as it will crack when rolled.
☐ Turn out onto sugared greaseproof paper. Remove lining paper and trim edges.
☐ Spread quickly with lightly warmed jam. Working from the narrow end roll with fingers then continue by drawing paper away from you over the sponge.
☐ Leave to cool resting on the seam. Dredge with caster sugar.

CHOCOLATE LOG
COOKING TIME 5 MINS
☐ Make a Swiss Roll but substitute 15g/½oz cocoa for 15g/½oz flour.
☐ When cooked roll up with a piece of grease proof paper instead of jam. Allow to cool then unroll.
☐ Remove paper and spread with chocolate butter cream. Mark with a fork and add decorations.

FRUIT CAKE
COOKING TIME 8 MINS
2×5ml spoon/2 teaspoons Baking Powder
125g/4oz Plain Flour
1×5ml spoon/1 teaspoon Mixed Spice
175g/6oz Dried Mixed Fruit
Pinch of Salt
75g/3oz Dark Brown Sugar
1×15ml spoon/1 tablespoon Milk
2× size 2/large eggs
75g/3oz butter

METHOD
☐ Put all ingredients except fruit in together and using an electric whisk mix for 2-3 minutes on slow speed or mix with a wooden spoon for 4 minutes.
☐ Lastly stir in fruit and put mixture in a 1.4-1.7 litres/2½-3 pint souffle dish, hollowing out the centre.
☐ Cook for 8 minutes on ROAST.
☐ Leave to stand.

CHERRY CAKE
COOKING TIME 9 MINS
125g/4oz Glace Cherries (chopped)
250g/8oz Self Raising Flour
125g/4oz Margarine
3× size 2/large eggs
Few drops of Vanilla Essence
125g/4oz caster sugar

milk to mix

METHOD
☐ Grease and line a cake dish, approximately 19cm/7½ inches in diameter.
☐ Wash cherries in water to remove syrup, and towel dry. Toss in some of the flour.
☐ Sift remaining flour into a bowl and rub in margarine. Add cherries and sugar mix in well.
☐ Beat together eggs, essence and a little milk, add to the cake mixture and mix with a fork until a soft batter is formed.
☐ Spread evenly in the dish and cook for 9 minutes on HIGH Leave to rest for 10 minutes before turning out.
☐ Sprinkle top with icing sugar.

ALL IN ONE VICTORIA SANDWICH
COOKING TIME 4-5 MINS
125g/4oz Soft Margarine
125g/4oz Caster Sugar
125g/4oz Self Raising Flour
2 Eggs
2×15ml spoon/2 tablespoons milk
Icing Sugar
Jam, Lemon Curd or Cream

METHOD
☐ Put all ingredients in a bowl and beat with a wooden spoon until smooth.
☐ Pour into prepared 8 inch cake dish and cook on HIGH for 4-5 minutes.
☐ Leave to stand for a few minutes.
☐ When cool split in half and fill with jam or cream or both and dredge with icing sugar.

PACKET CAKE MIX
COOKING TIME 4MINS
☐ Grease a cake dish or 20 cm/8 inch souffle dish.
☐ Make up as directed on packet and add an extra 2×15 ml spoon/tablespoons of water pour into prepared dish. Cook on HIGH for about 4 minutes.
☐ Test after 3½ minutes to see whether it springs back when lightly touched.
☐ Turn out and decorate in normal way.

CHRISTMAS CAKE
COOKING TIME 45 MINS
250 g/8 oz Butter
250 g/8 oz Dark Brown Sugar
4× size 2/large eggs
500 g/1 lb Currants
250 g/8 oz Raisins
250 g/8 oz Sultanas
50 g/2 oz Cherries, chopped
50 g/2 oz Chopped Peel, optional
50 g/2 oz Chopped Walnuts, optional
50 g/2 oz Shredded Almonds, optional
1×10 ml spoon/1 dessertspoon Black Treacle
1×5 ml spoon/1 teaspoon Vanilla Essence
1×2.5 ml spoon/½ teaspoon Ground Cinnamon
Pinch of Nutmeg
Pinch of Mixed Spice
150 g/5 oz Self Raising Flour
150 g/5 oz Plain Flour
Pinch Bicarbonate of Soda
Pinch Salt

METHOD
☐ Cream butter and sugar together until light and fluffy.
☐ Beat in eggs one at a time, adding a little flour with the last two eggs.
☐ Mix in treacle and essence.
☐ Sift dry ingredients together and add to creamed mixture and stir.
☐ Then add fruit and nuts.
☐ Put into a greased and lined 20 cm/8 inch round dish. Cook on DEFROST for 45 minutes.

GINGER CAKE
COOKING TIME 9 MINS
250 g/8 oz Self Raising Flour
1×5 ml spoon/1 teaspoon Ground Ginger
125 g/4 oz Butter or Margarine
125 g/4 oz Soft Dark Brown Sugar
50 g/2 oz Stem Ginger
1×15 ml spoon/1 tablespoon Ginger Syrup
2 Large Eggs
5×15 ml spoons/5 tablespoons Milk

METHOD
☐ Grease and line a round cake dish about 7½ inches in diameter.
☐ Sift flour and ginger in a bowl. Rub in margarine finely. Add the sugar and chopped ginger.
☐ Using a fork, mix to a soft batter with syrup, milk and eggs beaten together. Spoon into prepared dish and cook for 7 minutes on ROAST.
☐ Leave to rest for 15 minutes before turning out.
☐ When cooked sprinkle with icing sugar.

CHOCOLATE GATEAU
COOKING TIME 3-4 MINS
2 Eggs
50 g/2 oz Caster Sugar
37 g/1½ oz Self Raising Flour
12 g/½ oz Cocoa
Tin Mandarin Oranges or Black Cherries
300 ml/½ pint Fresh Double or Whipping Cream
Chocolate Bits

METHOD
☐ Whisk together eggs and sugar until thick, creamy and almost white in colour.
☐ Lightly fold sieved flour and cocoa into mixture with a metal spoon.
☐ Place in a well greased and lined 8 inch cake dish and cook on HIGH for 3-4 minutes. Leave to stand.
☐ When cool slice and spread with whipped cream and desired fruit.
☐ Cover sides with cream and roll in chocolate bits. Arrange rest of fruit on top and pipe on rest of cream.

← Victoria Sandwich

GINGERBREAD
COOKING TIME 8½ MINS
250g/8oz Self Raising Flour
Pinch Salt
2×5ml spoon/2 teaspoons Ground Ginger
50g/2oz Margarine
50g/2oz Dark Soft Brown Sugar
125g/4oz Black Treacle
1 Egg, and milk to make 150ml/¼ pint

METHOD
☐ Mix flour, salt and ginger together.
☐ In a dish put margarine, sugar and treacle. Cook on HIGH for 1½ minutes until melted, stir and add to the flour.
☐ Gradually beat in egg mixture. Stir until smooth, turn into 600ml/1 pint dish and cook on ROAST for 7 minutes.

BROWNIES
COOKING TIME 9 MINS
50g/2oz Plain Chocolate
75g/3oz Margarine
2 Eggs
150g/5oz Caster Sugar
125g/4oz Plain Flour
Pinch of Baking Powder
1×5ml spoon/1 teaspoon Vanilla Essence
1×15ml spoon/1 tablespoon Milk
50g/2oz Chopped Walnuts

METHOD
☐ Grease and line a suitable dish.
☐ Break chocolate into pieces and put into a basin with margarine. Melt on HIGH for 2 minutes. Stir.
☐ Beat eggs and sugar until smooth. Mix in flour, nuts, baking powder, essence and milk.
☐ Spread evenly into prepared dish and cook for 7 minutes on HIGH. Leave to stand for 10 minutes.
☐ Turn out and dust with icing sugar when cool.

CHOCOLATE RINGS
COOKING TIME 3 MINS
Makes about 25 rings
50g/2oz Margarine
50g/2oz Caster Sugar
½× size 4/small egg
Few drops vanilla essence
125g/4oz Plain Flour
125g/4oz Plain Chocolate, melted

METHOD
☐ Cream the margarine and sugar together.
☐ Beat in the eggs and essence.
☐ Work in the sieved flour.
☐ Knead lightly and then chill for 30 minutes.
☐ Roll out dough and cut into 6.5cm/2½ inch rounds. Remove centres with a smaller cutter.
☐ Cook 10 biscuits for 3 minutes on HIGH. Cool.
☐ Dip each ring into the melted chocolate to coat thoroughly and leave to set on a sheet of oiled greaseproof paper.

CHOCOLATE BUTTER ICING
COOKING TIME 1 MIN
65g/2½oz Margarine or Butter
3×15ml spoon/3 tablespoons Cocoa
275g/9oz Sieved Icing Sugar
3×15ml spoon/3 tablespoons Hot Milk
1×5ml spoon/1 teaspoon Vanilla Essence

METHOD
☐ Melt margarine on HIGH for 1 minute. Blend in cocoa.
☐ Stir in icing sugar, milk and essence. Beat until smooth and thick.

Brownies →

SHORTBREAD
COOKING TIME 5-7 MINS
150g/5oz Butter
125g/4oz Caster Sugar
300g/10oz Plain Flour

METHOD
☐ Cream the butter and sugar together until light and fluffy.
☐ Using a fork, work in the flour.
☐ Press into a 22.5cm/9 inch round lightly greased container. Cook on ROAST for 5-7 minutes.
☐ Leave to cool. Sprinkle with caster sugar and cut into fingers.

CARAMEL SHORTBREAD
COOKING TIME 14 MINS
1 Cooked Shortbread

FILLING
125g/4oz Butter
125g/4oz Caster Sugar
397g/14oz can condensed milk
2×15ml spoon/2 tablespoons Golden Syrup
125g/4oz Plain Chocolate

METHOD
☐ To prepare the filling, put all the ingredients into a large bowl and mix well. Cook on HIGH for 4 minutes until the sugar dissolves, then cook on HIGH for 8 minutes, stirring every two minutes.
☐ Pour onto cooked shortbread and leave to set.
☐ Break the chocolate into pieces in a bowl, microwave on HIGH for 2 minutes, until all the chocolate has melted, spread over the filling.
☐ Mark into fingers or squares and leave until cold and set before removing from the container.

FRUITY FLAPJACKS
COOKING TIME 4-5 MINS
75g/3oz Butter
75g/3oz Soft Brown Sugar
75g/3oz Porridge Oats
15g/½oz Mixed Nuts, chopped
25g/1oz Currants

METHOD
☐ Melt butter in a bowl for 1 minute on HIGH. Add remaining ingredients and mix well.
☐ Turn into a greased 18cm / 7 inch round shallow dish and press down well.
☐ Microwave on ROAST for 3-4 minutes until a cocktail stick inserted in the centre comes out cleanly.
☐ Leave in the dish to cool slightly. Then mark into wedges.
☐ Turn out onto a wire rack and cut into wedges when cold.

BRANDY SNAPS
COOKING TIME 2 MINS

Makes 12
50 g/2 oz Butter
50 g/2 oz Caster Sugar
75 g/3 oz Golden Syrup
1×5 ml spoon/1 teaspoon Lemon Juice
50 g/2 oz Plain Flour
1 level 5 ml spoon/1 level teaspoon
  Ground Ginger

METHOD
☐ Melt butter, sugar and syrup for
  2 minutes on HIGH.
☐ Add the lemon juice then add the
  sieved flour and ginger and mix well.
☐ Place 4 teaspoons of the mixture
  onto a well-greased plate or turntable.
  Cook for 2 minutes on HIGH.
☐ Remove from oven and leave to cool
  slightly until they are easily lifted.
☐ While still warm, wrap each one
  around a wooden spoon handle,
  working quickly. Allow to become firm
  before removing onto a wire tray.

CHOCOLATE KRISPIES
COOKING TIME 1 MIN

1½×15 ml spoon/1½ tablespoons Syrup
50 g/2 oz Butter
3×15 ml spoon/3 tablespoons Drinking
  Chocolate
100 g/3½ oz Rice Krispies

METHOD
☐ Put syrup and butter in a dish and
  cook on HIGH for 1 minute.
☐ Add chocolate and krispies and mix
  well.
☐ Place small amounts in paper cases
  and leave to set.

NOTE:
These can be made with cornflakes instead
of rice krispies.

FLORENTINES
COOKING TIME 3½ MINS

Makes 16-18
125 g/4 oz Butter
125 g/4 oz Soft Brown Sugar
1×15 ml spoon/1 tablespoon Golden Syrup
125 g/4 oz Blanched Chopped Almonds
25 g/1 oz Glace Cherries, chopped
25 g/1 oz Walnuts, chopped
25 g/1 oz Sultanas, chopped
25 g/1 oz Candied Peel/cut mixed peel

COATING
75 g/3 oz Plain Chocolate, melted

METHOD
☐ Melt butter, sugar and syrup in a bowl
  on HIGH for 2 minutes.
☐ Stir in the rest of ingredients and mix
  well.
☐ Put 4 small teaspoons of the mixture
  onto a well-greased baking tray
  suitable for a microwave (plate will do)
  or turntable, allowing plenty of space
  for the biscuits to spread out. Cook
  on HIGH for 1½ minutes.
☐ When cooked, cool slightly, then lift
  carefully onto a cooling tray.
☐ When cool, coat the base of the
  florentines with melted chocolate.

HOW SWEET IT IS!

Desserts can transform a simple meal into a delectable feast. From baked fresh fruit to fudgy chocolate cake, they make the perfect ending to any meal. Here are some traditional family favorites, glamorous party desserts, and spur-of-the-moment treats. All are quick and easy with your microwave oven. In no time at all, cakes will rise before your eyes, custards will become thick and creamy, and pie fillings will bubble and thicken. And if you've never tried home-made sweets, now is the time! It's impossible to fail when you make them the microwave way.

Yellow food coloring added to Homemade Pie Shell will enhance the appearance. Rice Chocolate fudge is easy. A sweet thermometer is used in the first step (top right) then other ingredients are added (above left). Microwave cakes rise higher than conventional. Fill cake pans only half-full (above right).

Converting Your Recipes

How easy it is! Puddings and custards can be baked without the usual water bath, and they need only occasional stirring. Fruits retain their bright colour and fresh-picked flavour. Cakes cook so quickly; yet they are superior in texture, taste, and height. When you discover how effortless it is to make desserts, you'll be trying all those recipes you've been longing to do. Because cakes and pie crusts cook so fast, they do not brown. If you like a browned surface, there are many ways to give desserts a browned look. So try adapting your dessert recipes following the guidance of a similar recipe here and these tips:

☐ You can enhance your light batter cookies and cakes with cinnamon, nutmeg, brown sugar, coffee, nuts, toppings, frostings, glazes, food coloring, etc.

☐ Layer cakes are generally baked one layer at a time. Baking is usually begun on simmer or bake for the first 7 minutes, then finished on HIGH. If cake appears to be rising unevenly, rotate the dish one-quarter turn as necessary. Denser batters, such as fruit cakes and carrot cakes, require slower, gentler cooking. Set at 30 (defrost) for good results.

☐ All pies should be made in glass pie plates so you will be able to check the bottom for readiness.

☐ A pie shell is cooked when very slight browning occurs on top, and surface appears opaque and dry.

☐ For even cooking, select fruit of uniform size to be cooked whole, as in baked apples, or to be cooked in pieces, as in apple pie.

☐ Remove baked custards from oven when centeres are nearly firm. They will continue to cook and set after removal.

☐ To avoid lumping, puddings should be stirred once or twice during the second half of cooking.

COOKING GUIDE—PUDDING AND PIE FILLING MIX

Food	Amount	Time (in minutes)	Cook Control Setting	Special Notes
Pudding and pie filling mix	3¼ ounces	6½-7	HIGH	Follow package directions. Stir every 3 minutes.
	5½ ounces	8-10	HIGH	Use 4-cup glass measure.
Egg custard	3 ounces	8-10	Roast	Follow package direction. Stir every 3 minutes. Use 4-cup glass measure.
Tapioca	3¼ ounces	6-7	HIGH	Follow package directions. Stir every 3 minutes. Use 4-cup glass measure.

COOKING/DEFROSTING GUIDE—CONVENIENCE DESSERTS

Food	Amount	Cook Control Setting	Time	Special Notes
Brownies, other bars, frozen	12-13 oz.	Defrost	2-3 minutes	In origial ¾" foil tray, lid removed. Let stand 5 minutes.
Cookies, frozen	6	Defrost	50-60 seconds	Place on paper plate or towels.
Pineapple upside-down cake mix.	21½ oz.	Simmer HIGH	3 minutes 4 minutes	Use 9" round glass dish. Remove enough batter for 2 cupcakes, bake separately. Rotate if rising unevenly.
Cupcakes or crumb cakes, frozen	1 or 2	Defrost	½-1 minute	Place on shallow plate.
Cheesecake, frozen	17-19 oz.	Defrost	4-5 minutes	Remove from foil pan to plate. Let stand 1 minute.
Pound cake, frozen	10¾ oz.	Defrost	2 minutes	Remove from foil pan to plate. Rotate once. Let stand 5 minutes.
Cake, frozen 2- or 3-layer	17 oz.	Defrost	2½-3 minutes	Remove from foil pan to plate. Watch carefully, frosting melts fast. Let stand 5 minutes.
Custard pie, frozen	9" pie	Roast	4-5½ minutes	Remove from foil pan to plate. Centre should be nearly set.
Fruit pie, frozen, unbaked, 2 crusts	9" pie	HIGH	13-15 minutes	On glass pie plate. Brown, if desired, in preheated 425° conventional oven 8-10 minutes.
Frozen fruit	10 oz.	HIGH	5-5½ minutes	On microproof plate. Slit pouch. Flex halfway through cooking time to mix.
	16 oz.	HIGH	7-9 minutes	Remove from bag. Place in glass casserole, cover. Stir halfway through cooking time.

HONEYCOMB
COOKING TIME 12 MINS
3×15ml spoon/3 tablespoons Clear Honey
5×15ml spoon/5 tablespoons Sugar
4×15ml spoon/4 tablespoons Water
15g/½oz Butter
1×2.5ml spoon/½ teaspoon Vinegar
1×2.5ml spoon/½ teaspoon Bicarbonate of Soda

METHOD
☐ Put honey, sugar, water, butter and vinegar into a large bowl. Heat on HIGH for 3 minutes (until the sugar dissolves).
☐ Cover and bring to the boil by cooking for 1 minute on HIGH. Stir.
☐ Cook for 8 minutes on ROAST or until a teaspoon of the mixture dropped into a cup of cold water separates into hard and brittle threads.
☐ Stir in bicarbonate of soda and pour into a greased tin.
☐ When set, break into pieces.

COCONUT ICE
COOKING TIME 18-20 MINS
750g/1½lb Granulated Sugar
300ml/½ pint Water
2 pinches Cream of Tartar
250g/8oz Dessicated Coconut
Pink Colouring

METHOD
☐ Grease a square tin well.
☐ Combine sugar, water and cream of tartar and cook covered for 18-20 minutes on HIGH, until a teaspoon of the mixture forms a soft ball when dropped in cold water.
☐ Remove. Stir in coconut, spread half into prepared tin.
☐ Add a few drops of pink colouring to the remainder and spread over the first layer.
☐ When cool cut into squares.

NOTE:
For chocolate coconut ice add 1×10ml spoon/1 dessert spoon cocoa and a drop of vanilla essence instead of pink colouring.

PEPPERMINT CREAMS
COOKING TIME 1½ MINS
50g/2oz Butter
2×15ml spoon/2 tablespoons Milk
1×5ml spoon/1 teaspoon Peppermint
  Essence
500g/1lb Icing Sugar
Green Colouring
Icing Sugar for kneading

METHOD
☐ Melt butter on HIGH for 1 minute.
  Add the milk and essence.
☐ Warm for 30 seconds on HIGH.
☐ Add the icing sugar and mix well.
☐ Knead on a board dusted with icing
  sugar. Roll out and cut out with a
  small pastry cutter. Leave to cool.
☐ If desired half the mixture can be
  coloured by kneading a few drops of
  green colouring.

FUDGE
COOKING TIME 30 MINS
500g/1lb Sugar
300ml/½ pint Milk
125g/4oz Butter
2×5ml spoon/2 teaspoons Vanilla Essence
125g/4oz Plain Chocolate Drops

METHOD
☐ Combine sugar, milk and butter in a
  dish. Cook covered for 30 minutes
  on ROAST stirring frequently until a
  teaspoon of the mixture forms a ball
  when dropped into cold water.
☐ Remove from oven, stir in essence
  and leave to cool for 5 minutes.
☐ Beat until thick and creamy.
☐ Add the chocolate drops and pour
  into a greased 18cm/7 inch square
  tin.
☐ Mark into squares, cut when firm
  and set.

VARIATIONS
Cherry
Follow recipe but add 50g/2oz glace
cherries instead of chocolate drops.
Walnut
Add 50g/2oz chopped walnuts instead of
chocolate drops.
Raisin
Add 50g/2oz seedless raisins instead of
chocolate drops.

CREME CARAMEL
COOKING TIME 29 MINS
FOR THE CUSTARD
600ml/1 pint Milk
25g/1oz Sugar
4× size 3/standard egg

FOR THE CARAMEL
125g/4oz Sugar
150ml/¼ pint Water

METHOD
☐ Heat the milk for 3 minutes on HIGH.
☐ Beat the eggs with the sugar and
  pour the milk over.
☐ Place the sugar and water in a suitable
  container. Heat for 5 minutes on
  HIGH, then stir and heat on HIGH for
  a further 9 minutes.
☐ Strain the custard mixture into the
  container and place the dish in a
  shallow water bath in the oven and
  cook on ROAST for 12 minutes.
☐ Leave to stand before serving.

RUM TRUFFLES
COOKING TIME 2 MINS
125g/4oz Plain Chocolate
50g/2oz Butter
1×5ml spoon/1 teaspoon Rum
2 Egg Yolks
50g/2oz Stale Cake Crumbs
250g/8oz Icing Sugar, Sifted
Chocolate Vermicelli

METHOD
☐ Place the chocolate and butter in a bowl and cook on HIGH for 2 minutes. Stir occasinally.
☐ Add rum and egg yolks and beat well.
☐ Add cake crumbs and icing sugar and mix well.
☐ Roll into small balls and roll in the chocolate vermicelli.
☐ Instead of using rum in truffles any favourite spirits can be substituted.
☐ Transfer to sweet cases.

MILLES FEUILLES
COOKING TIME 4 MINS
1 Packet (250g/8oz) Frozen Puff Pastry
6×15ml spoon/6 tablespoons strawberry jam
300ml/½ pint Double Cream, whipped
75g/3oz Icing Sugar

METHOD
☐ Leave pastry to thaw at room temperature.
☐ Divide the pastry into 2 pieces. Roll each piece into an oblong, 20cm/ 8 inches by 10cm/4 inches.
☐ Cook each piece separately on a sheet of greaseproof paper for 4 minutes on HIGH. Split into two and leave to cool.
☐ Sandwich the pastry together with layers of the jam and cream.
☐ Sift the icing sugar on top. Serve cut in slices.

STRAWBERRY CHEESECAKE
COOKING TIME 32-37 MINS·
250g/8oz Ginger Biscuits, crushed
125g/4oz Butter or Margarine

FILLING
500g/1 lb Curd Cheese
125g/4oz Caster Sugar
1× size 2/large egg
25g/1oz Sultanas, optional
Grated rind of one lemon
Milk to glaze
Whipped cream & Strawberries to decorate

METHOD
☐ Grease an 20cm/8 inch Microwave proof dish.
☐ Melt the butter or magarine in a bowl for 2 minutes on HIGH.
☐ Add the crushed biscuits, mix together, and press into the bottom and sides of the dish. Chill until firm.
☐ Mix all the ingredients for the filling together and beat for 1-2 minutes. Place in the crumb case and brush with milk.
☐ Cook on SIMMER for 30-35 minutes, until the centre is almost set.
☐ Allow to cool completely and then turn out. Decorate with whipped cream and strawberries.

BAKEWELL TART
COOKING TIME 2½-3 MINS
1 prepared pastry case

FILLING
Jam
50g/2oz Margarine
50g/2oz Caster Sugar
50g/2oz Self Raising Flour
1 Egg

METHOD
☐ Cover base of pastry with a little jam.
☐ Cream together margarine and sugar.
☐ Fold in beaten egg and flour. Pour into pastry case, cook for 2½-3 minutes on HIGH.

Strawberry Cheese Cake ➙

APPLE CRISP
COOKING TIME 7½ MINS

750g/1½lb cooking apples, peeled, cored and sliced
75g/3oz granulated sugar
150g/5½oz digestive or ginger biscuits
50g/2oz butter
50g/2oz demerara sugar

METHOD
☐ Arrange layers of apple and sugar alternately in a pie dish.
☐ Crush the biscuits with a rolling pin.
☐ Melt the butter for 30 seconds on HIGH.
☐ Add the crushed biscuits and demerara sugar and mix together thoroughly.
☐ Place over the apple and spread evenly. Cook on HIGH for 7 minutes.
☐ Serve with cream or custard.

SPICEY APPLE PIE
COOKING TIME 18-20 MINS

500g/1lb Cooking Apples
125g/4oz Sugar
2×15ml spoon/2 tablespoons Flour
Pinch Salt
1×2.5ml spoon/½ teaspoon Cinnamon
1×1.25ml spoon/¼ teaspoon ground nutmeg
1×5ml spoon/1 teaspoon Lemon Juice
15g/½oz Butter

PASTRY
250g/8oz Plain Flour
50g/2oz Lard
50g/2oz Margarine
Pinch Salt
1×15ml spoon/1 tablespoon Water
Little Yellow Food Colouring

METHOD
☐ Peel and core apples. Mix in a bowl with sugar, flour, salt, cinnamon and nutmeg.
☐ Make up pastry by rubbing fat into flour and salt. Add the water with added colouring one tablespoon at a time.
☐ Roll out half and line a pie dish or plate.
☐ Place apples on top and sprinkle with lemon juice. Dot with butter.
☐ Roll out remainder of pastry and fit over the top. Seal edges and cut slits in the top.
☐ Cook uncovered for on HIGH 8 minutes until apples are soft.
☐ While apples are cooking, preheat conventional oven to 400°F 200°C or gas No. 6.
☐ When apples are cooling, bake in oven for 10-12 minutes until crust is golden brown.
☐ Sprinkle with sugar. Serve with fresh cream. To get a nice glaze brush with beaten egg before baking in conventional oven.

PASTRY FLAN CASE
COOKING TIME 5 MINS

125g/4oz Plain Flour
Pinch Salt
25g/1oz Lard
25g/1oz Margarine
2×15ml spoon/2 tablespoons Water

METHOD
☐ Sift flour and salt together in a bowl. Rub in fat.
☐ Tint water with a few drops of yellow food colouring. Add liquid to mixture one tablespoon at a time to form a smooth dough. Knead into shape.
☐ Roll out to fit an average flan dish. Flute edges and trim.
☐ Prick base and place a piece of absorbent kitchen paper over the pastry and place a plate on top.
☐ Cook on HIGH for 3 minutes.
☐ Remove plate and paper and continue cooking for a further 2 minutes until pastry is cooked in the centre.

Spice Apple Pie →

LEMON MERINGUE PIE
COOKING TIME 6 MINS
1 pastry case cooked

FILLING
2 Eggs, separated
250g/8oz Caster Sugar
Juice and grated rind of 1 lemon
150ml/¼ pint Water
25g/1oz Cornflour

METHOD
☐ Beat egg yolks with half of the sugar, add lemon juice and rind. Set aside.
☐ Boil water on HIGH for 2 minutes, add to egg mixture and stir.
☐ Put back in oven and cook on HIGH for 1½ minutes until boiling.
☐ Blend in cornflour, mix to a smooth paste with a little cold water.
☐ Heat on HIGH for 2½ minutes stirring every 30 seconds. Pour into cooked flan case.
☐ Whisk egg whites stiffly, gradually beat in remaining sugar. Spread over flan and put under a hot grill for a few minutes until lightly brown.

FRUIT FLAN
COOKING TIME 3 MINS
1 Pastry Case prepared and cooked

FILLING
Fruit: Fresh, canned or frozen.
Arrowroot glaze: 1½×5ml spoon/
   1½ teaspoons arrowroot
150ml/¼ pint Water

METHOD
☐ Fill pastry case with desired fruit and make up glaze by blending arrowroot with a little liquid.
☐ Place remaining liquid in microwave and cook on HIGH for 2 minutes until boiling.
☐ Pour onto arrowroot. Stir, return to oven and cook for another 1 minute stirring every 20 seconds until mixture clears.
☐ Pour over flan and decorate with cream and angelica.

MICROWAVE CUSTARD TART
COOKING TIME 11½ MINS
1 prepared pastry case

FILLING
2 Eggs
300ml/½ pint Milk
2×15ml spoon/2 tablespoons Sugar
Small piece of Vanilla Pod or 0.25ml
   spoon/¼ teaspoon Vanilla Essence
Grated Nutmeg

METHOD
☐ Whisk eggs. Bring milk, vanilla and sugar to boil by cooking on HIGH for 4½ minutes.
☐ Pour onto eggs and cool. Remove vanilla pod.
☐ Strain through a sieve into prepared flan case, and sprinkle with grated nutmeg.
☐ Cook on ROAST for 4 minutes. Leave to stand for 5 minutes then cook again on ROAST for 2 minutes.
☐ Leave to stand to finish cooking.

NOTE:
To make custard tarlets line small cups with the pastry and fill individually.

CHERRY AND ALMOND PUDDING
COOKING TIME 6 MINS
2×15ml spoon/2 tablespoons Golden Syrup
425g/15oz can of Cherries, pitted and
   drained
25g/1oz Margarine
25g/1oz Caster Sugar
75g/3oz Self Raising Flour
25g/1oz Ground Almonds
1×2.5ml spoon/½ teaspoon Almond
   Essence
2 Eggs
1×15ml spoon/1 tablespoon Milk

METHOD
☐ Grease a 17.5-18cm/8 inch dish

- Place the golden syrup on the base of the dish. Then place a layer of cherries on top.
- Mix all the remaining ingredients together for 2-3 minutes and place on top of the cherries. Even out and cover.
- Cook for 6 minutes on HIGH.
- Leave to stand for 5 minutes before serving with cream or custard.

JAM-CAP PUDDING
COOKING TIME 5 MINS
3×15ml spoon/3 tablespoons Jam
125g/4oz Self Raising Flour
50g/2oz Shredded Suet
50g/2oz Caster Sugar
1×5ml spoon/1 teaspoon Vanilla Essence or flavouring
1 Egg (standard), beaten
6×15ml spoons/6 tablespoons Milk

METHOD
- Grease a 900ml/1½ pint Pudding basin. Place the jam in the base.
- Sift the flour into a bowl. Add the suet and sugar. Mix ingredients together.
- Using a fork, mix the other ingredients to a soft batter. Stir, do not beat.
- Pour into prepared basin. Cover with cling film, puncturing to prevent it from "ballooning" up in oven.
- Cook on HIGH for 5 minutes.
- Take out of oven, leave to stand for 5 minutes before removing film and inverting pudding onto a plate.
- Serve with cream or custard.

SYRUP LAYER PUDDING
COOKING TIME 5½ MINS
250g/8oz Self Raising Flour
Pinch of Salt
75g/3oz Suet
Approx. 150ml/¼ pint Water
6-7×15ml spoon/6-7 tablepoons Golden Syrup

METHOD
- Sieve flour and salt together. Stir in the suet, mix to a soft dough with the water.
- Grease a 1.1 litre 2 pint/pudding basin.
- Divide pastry into 4 unequal portions.
- Roll out the smallest piece and place on the base of the basin. Spread with some of syrup.
- Continue in this way and finish with a layer of pastry.
- Cover and cook on HIGH for 5½ minutes.
- Leave to stand for 5 minutes before inverting pudding onto a plate.
- Serve with cream or custard.

NOTE:
Jam or mincemeat can be substituted for syrup.

QUICK ORANGE STEAMED PUDDING
COOKING TIME 5 MINS
125g/4oz Butter, soft margarine
125g/4oz Caster Sugar
125g/4oz Self Raising Flour
2× size 3/standard eggs
Finely Grated Rind and Juice of 1 Orange

METHOD
- Mix all ingredients together and beat for 2-3 minutes.
- Place in a 1.2 litre/2 pint greased pudding basin.
- Cover and cook on HIGH for 5 minutes.
- Leave to stand for 5 minutes before serving.
- Serve with golden syrup.

JAM ROLY-POLY
COOKING TIME 5 MINS
125g/4oz Self Raising Flour
Pinch of Salt
50g/2oz Shredded Suet
2-3×15ml spoons/2-3 tablespoons Hot
   Water
6×15ml spoons/6 tablespoons Jam

METHOD
☐ Sift the flour and salt into a mixing
   bowl. Stir in the suet, and then
   gradually add the hot water until the
   dough comes together. Knead lightly
   until smooth. Roll out on a floured
   board in an oblong shape about.
   75mm/¼ inch thick/about 9½
   inches×7 inches 24cm×17cm.
☐ Spread half the jam along the dough,
   leaving about 1.25cm/½ inch gap
   along edges.
☐ Roll up like a swiss roll, sealing the
   edges with a little water.
☐ Place in an oblong dish (pie dish will
   do) and cover.
☐ Cook on HIGH for 5 minutes.
☐ Just before serving, reheat the
   remaining jam and pour over the
   roly-poly.

NOTE:
Marmalade, mincemeat can be substituted
for the jam.

BAKED APPLES
COOKING TIME 8 MINS
4 Medium Sized Cooking Apples
50g/2oz Mixed dried fruit & Glace Cherries
25g/1oz Brown Sugar
4×5ml spoon/4 teaspoons Golden Syrup

METHOD
☐ Remove cores from apples with corer.
☐ Pierce all around the skin half-way
   down apple.
☐ Place in a shallow container and fill
   the centre with fruit and sugar. Pour
   1×5ml/1 teaspoon golden syrup
   over each apple.
☐ Cook on HIGH for 8 minutes.

PINEAPPLE UPSIDE DOWN PUDDING
COOKING TIME 5-6 MINS
125g/4oz Margarine
125g/4oz Caster Sugar
125g/4oz Self Raising Flour
2× size 3/standard eggs
227g/8oz Pineapple Rings and 2×15ml
   spoon/2 tablespoons Pineapple Juice.
Glace Cherries
Brown Sugar

METHOD
☐ Grease a cake dish with melted butter
   and sprinkle with brown sugar.
☐ Place the drained pineapple rings
   and cherries in the bottom.
☐ Cream together Margarine and sugar
   until white and fluffy. Beat in eggs and
   flour alternately. Beat in Pineapple
   Juice.
☐ Spread mixture over the pineapples
   and smooth over. Cook on HIGH for
   5-6 minutes.
☐ When time has finished leave cake to
   stand for another 1 minute. Leave to
   cool then turn out.

PEARS IN WINE
COOKING TIME 15½ MINS
125g/4oz Sugar
150ml/¼ pint Water
150ml/¼ pint Red Wine
1 strip Lemon Rind
1×2.5ml spoon/½ teaspoon Ground
   Cinnamon
6 Medium Pears
25g/1oz Toasted Flaked Almonds

METHOD
☐ Place the sugar, water, wine, lemon
   rind and cinnamon in a large bowl
   and heat until the sugar dissolves,
   about 2½ minutes on HIGH.
☐ Peel the pears, cutting off the core at
   the base and leaving the stalks on.

- Add to the bowl, cover and cook for about 8 minutes on HIGH turning once.
- Remove the pears and stand upright in a serving dish.
- Boil the liquid in the dish until it thickens and is syrupy, about 5 minutes on HIGH.
- Allow to cool slightly. Remove the lemon rind, then pour over the pears.
- When the pears and syrup are cold, chill in the refrigerator for a couple of hours, spooning the syrup over the pears from time to time. Before serving, sprinkle over the almonds.

FLAMING APPLES
COOKING TIME 18 MINS
4 Dessert Apples
Lemon Juice
1×5 ml spoon/1 teaspoon Cinnamon
175 g/6 oz Soft Brown Sugar
900 ml/1½ pints Boiling Water
3×15 ml spoon/3 tablespoons Rum

METHOD
- Peel the apples, without removing the stalks. Dip the apples into the lemon juice to prevent discolouration.
- Place the sugar, cinnamon and water in a large container. Cook on HIGH for 2 minutes or until all the sugar has dissolved.
- Add the apples and cook on HIGH for 7 minutes or until just tender. Drain, remove and place in a serving dish.
- Boil the syrup on HIGH until the syrup begins to thicken, about 8 minutes.
- Pour the syrup, then the rum over the apples and microwave on HIGH for 1 minute.
- Ignite and serve immediately.

LEMON SOUFFLE
COOKING TIME 30 SECONDS
1 envelope gelatine
3×15 ml spoon/3 tablespoons Hot Water
Yolks and Whites of 2 Eggs
50 g/2 oz Caster Sugar
Finely Grated Rind and Juice of 1 Medium Sized Lemon
150 ml/¼ pint Double Cream

DECORATION
37 g/1½ oz Chopped Nuts
Whipped Fresh Cream
Angelica

METHOD
- Tie a collar of greased greaseproof paper around a ½ litre (1 pint) souffle dish, making sure paper stands 4-5cm (1½-2 inches) above edge of dish.
- Place the gelatine and water in a glass and heat on HIGH for about 30 seconds.
- Whisk the egg yolks and sugar together until thick and pale. Gently whisk in dissolved gelatine, lemon rind and juice.
- Leave to cool, until just beginning to thicken and set at edges.
- Meanwhile whisk the cream until lightly stiff. Beat egg whites until a stiff snow.
- Gently fold lemon mixture into cream. Fold in beaten egg whites.
- Pour into the prepared souffle dish and leave to set.
- Before serving remove the paper and gently press chopped nuts against side of souffle. Decorate top with whipped cream and Angelica.

STRAWBERRY MOUSSE
COOKING TIME 30 SECONDS
250g/8oz Strawberries
140g/4¾oz Strawberry Jelly
300ml/½ pint Water
2 Egg Whites
150ml/¼ pint Double Cream, whipped

METHOD
☐ Melt jelly in microwave for 30 seconds on HIGH. Add water and stir until well blended.
☐ Place in fridge and leave until just beginning to set around the edges.
☐ Puree strawberries and stir into jelly.
☐ Whisk egg whites until stiff and stir into strawberry mixture, then finally, stir in whipped cream.
☐ Put into serving dish and refrigerate until completely set.
☐ Decorate with whipped cream before serving.

CHOCOLATE MOUSSE
COOKING TIMES 2-3 MINS
125g/4oz Plain Chocolate
4 Eggs, separated
Whipped Cream for decoration

METHOD
☐ Break the chocolate into pieces and place in a bowl. Melt for 2-3 minutes on HIGH in the microwave.
☐ Stir in the egg yolks and mix well. Leave to cool.
☐ Beat the egg whites until stiff enough to stand in peaks, then fold in to the chocolate mixture.
☐ Pour the mousse into 4 individual serving dishes and leave until set.
☐ Decorate with the whipped cream.

FRUIT MOUSSE
COOKING TIME 30 SECONDS
150ml Fruit Puree, raspberries, blackberries etc.
25g/1oz Caster Sugar
2×5ml spoon/2 teaspoons Lemon Juice
3×5ml spoon/3 teaspoons Gelatine
2×15ml spoon/2 tablespoons Fruit Juice or Water
125ml/¼ pint Double Cream
2 Egg Whites
Colouring if required
Whipped Cream—optional

METHOD
☐ Put the puree, sugar and lemon juice into a bowl.
☐ Put the gelatine and fruit juice/water into a cup and heat for 30 seconds.
☐ Whisk the cream until it leaves a trail.
☐ Add the gelatine to the puree. Fold in the cream and colour if necessary.
☐ Whisk the egg whites until stiff and fold into the mixture.
☐ Pour or spoon into a serving dish. Leave to set.
☐ Decorate with whipped cream.
☐ Serve with Langues de Chat.

← Chocolate Mousse

INDEX